New England Seacoast Adventures

New England Seacoast Adventures

A COMPLETE GUIDE TO OUTDOOR RECREATION FROM CONNECTICUT TO MAINE

Stephen Jermanok

The Countryman Press
Woodstock, Vermont

Library of Congress Cataloging-in-Publication Data

Jermanok, Stephen.
    New England seacoast adventures : a complete guide to outdoor
  recreation from Connecticut to Maine / Stephen Jermanok.— 1st ed.
       p.   cm.
  Includes index.
  ISBN 0-88150-510-2
    1. Outdoor recreation—New England—Guidebooks. 2. Coasts—New
England—Recreational use—Guidebooks. 3. New England—Guidebooks.
I. Title.

GV191.42.N3 J47 2002
917.404'44—dc21

                               2002024495

Cover photo ©Rob Bossi
Cover design by Johnson Design
Text design by Chelsea Cloeter
Interior photos by Stephen Jermanok

Published by The Countryman Press, P.O. Box 748,
Woodstock, Vermont 05091

Distributed by W.W. Norton & Company, Inc.,
500 Fifth Avenue, New York, NY 10110

Printed in the United States of America

10 9 8 7 6 5 4 3 2 1

Contents

Acknowledgments

▶ This book would never have come to fruition without the keen advice and wise guidance from the following people. First and foremost, my wife, Lisa, who accompanied me on many of these trips or took care of our children, five-year-old Jake and three-year-old Melanie, while I was off walking the beach. I'm grateful to my brother Jim, who kept me laughing on numerous hiking, biking, sea kayaking, and fishing adventures; Fawn, Jack, Sarah, and Max for keeping me company in Cape Ann; Julie, Neil, Ami, and Tali for our week together in Maine; Julio and Ginny for sailing with me in Maine; and Fran for her continuing support of my career. Kudos go to Charlene Williams and Nancy Marshall on the Maine chapters, Jean Hebert in Connecticut, Becky Bovell in Rhode Island, and Amy Strack in Massachusetts. Thanks to my editor, Kermit Hummel, for having the patience to deal with my crazed schedule. Also to my agent, Lisa Hagen, for finding the perfect home for this book. Finally, I would like to thank all the park rangers, outfitters, sporting goods store owners, friends, and anonymous lovers of the outdoors who helped me along the way.

Introduction

▶ I grew up less than an hour's drive from one of the largest parks in America, the Adirondacks, and wilderness to me was always a deep-in-the-woods trail or a placid pond to paddle. Our yearly jaunt to the coast, usually Cape Cod, was a chance to practice my miniature golf swing or see how many licks it takes to get to the middle of a soft-serve ice-cream cone. Then it was off to the beach to lather on the lotion and slip onto the only speck of sand not yet covered with a beach blanket. Little did I realize that less than 15 minutes away from those overcrowded dunes was a 2-mile walk on untrammeled coastline that had fewer people than many of my Adirondack hikes. Or that the advent of sea kayaking would take me even farther away from civilization, suspended halfway in the ocean, head inches away from the water line.

For the past 15 years, I've had the good fortune to live in Manhattan and Boston, the two largest urban areas closest to the New England coast. Perhaps as a result of living in large cities, I've come to appreciate the natural splendor of this varied coastline that much more: from the shallow beaches of Connecticut's Long Island Sound to the rolling dunes of the Cape Cod National Seashore to the rugged granite shores of Maine's long stretch of coast. Sure, I still stop for ice cream and a game of putt-putt, but most of the time I'm savoring the wilderness, yes the wilderness, of this special part of the country.

I've kayaked with seals in the ocean waters around Cape Ann, cycled lonely back roads on Martha's Vineyard, and climbed up the only mountains on the Atlantic coast north of Brazil, in Acadia National Park. I found a beach on the Cape Cod National Seashore that isn't wall-to-wall people when it's 96 degrees in the shade, chartered a sailboat in Rhode Island to cruise to Block Island, and went on a deep-woods walk in Connecticut within an hour's drive of New York City.

Now it's your turn. Finally there's a definitive guide to the premier summer outdoor activities on the New England coast. No longer will you have to purchase separate books on every sport and every region in New England. This book is all-encompassing, covering the New England coast from Greenwich, Connecticut, to Eastport, Maine. It includes every warm-weather sport imaginable, from walking to biking to fishing to hiking to canoeing, swimming, and beachcombing. Most importantly, this guide is for everyone. I don't care if you're an average Joe who yearns to play outdoors, a parent like me who has small children, a cyclist training to be the next Lance Armstrong, or a couch potato who wishes to leave home to cool off at a beach on a hot summer's day. You'll find a long list of invigorating activities to choose from. All you need is the desire to venture outdoors into America's most historic and majestic region.

This book is divided into six geographical regions. Each regional chapter includes an in-depth list of sports, categorized alphabetically. Under each sport's heading, I feature specific trails, routes, and waterways that I personally tried and found to be the best. These featured activities are described in detail, including time required, level of difficulty, and location. Of course, time and level of difficulty are relative terms, but I have based these estimates on the average person who exercises several times a week and is in halfway decent shape. At the end of each chapter, I recommend places to camp.

These paths, routes, and waterways were not chosen at random. During the past year, I have talked with park rangers, outfitters, sporting goods store owners, high school and college coaches, members of sporting clubs, professional athletes, family members, friends, and locals who have lived their entire lives in New England. I somehow managed, by the power of persuasion or by simply prying, to get these people to reveal their most coveted trails, fishing holes, and backcountry roads. No one could possibly know these places unless they lived in these locales for years. Now they appear in print for the first time.

Next came the fun part. With my treasured list of recommended activities, I hiked the trails, walked the beaches, biked the rolling roads, and mountain biked on secluded forest trails. More than half of these routes never made it into this book. They were good exercise, but for one reason or another, I did not feel that they were the premier trips on the New England coast. Thus, I can attest to the high quality of every one of the featured trails in this book. These trips are indeed the best New England has to offer.

Place a copy of *New England Seacoast Adventures* in the glove compartment and follow me to the locales I've come to cherish—places the crowds couldn't know unless they scoured the coastline pestering the locals like I have.

CHAPTER ONE
Connecticut

▶ If you've ever traveled on Interstate 95 along the Connecticut coast, you've undoubtedly encountered the ebb and flow of traffic that never seems to cease. Well, congestion is nothing new in New England's southernmost state. When the first wave of immigrants arrived in the New World, they searched for a land that was both fertile and accessible. Heading southwest by boat from Massachusetts, they arrived at the shores of Connecticut, excited by the prospects of the terrain. The settlers found the mouth of the Connecticut River and immediately headed inland, where large tracts of rich soil were waiting at the bottom of the valley. Farmers began to grow corn, rye, oats, barley, and the vegetables that became an important part of the Colonial diet.

Families prospered, and the population grew. By 1700, there were eighty thousand people living in the low-lying areas along the coast and up the central valley. Writer Thomas Pownall stated that by 1776, the land between New Haven and Hartford was "a rich, well cultivated Vale thickly settled and swarming with people . . . It is as though you were still traveling along one continued town for 70 or 80 miles on end." The bulk of this population explosion was not the result of new immigrants, but of large families. In a pamphlet titled *Population in Eighteenth Century Connecticut,* Albert Laverne Olson wrote, "Travelers passing houses frequently noticed ten or twelve little heads peeping out of doors and windows... Eight to twenty children to a family were not uncommon."

Today, with a population that exceeds 3 million, Connecticut is often viewed as a small industrialized state with sprawling suburbs. This is especially true of the southwest corner, with its combination of small cities like Stamford and Bridgeport and wealthy communities like Greenwich and Westport, where men and women line up every morning to catch the Metro-North train to New York City. However, there is another Connecticut: a Connecticut with long stretches of sand and expansive views of the sea, a state where backcountry roads roll over the hills, laced by 200-year-old stone walls.

Connecticut is often overlooked by outdoors enthusiasts in favor of its neighbors farther north. If you haven't been here recently, it deserves a second look. Come surf-cast in Long Island Sound for striped bass and bluefish, bring your bikes for a pastoral pedal in the hills or along the shores, take a stroll on undeveloped coastline, or simply lounge on one of numerous town beaches or state parks that are perfectly situated at the water. Better yet, get out on the water via sea kayak or sailboat and have the shores to yourself on one of the Norfolk or Thimble Islands—even if it's only for an hour-long break from the white-knuckle driving on I-95.

THE TERRAIN

The mighty glacier that formed notches of granite in the White Mountains and thousands of islands, coves, and rocky promontories along the Maine coast brought relatively little change to eastern Connecticut. There's the occasional glacier detritus like the large boulders found at Glacial Park near Groton, but generally, the shores of Connecticut are a combination of soft sand and little surf. Beaches, bays, salt marshes, and rocky headlands form the shoreline, which is protected from the open sea by Long Island and the Sound. Heading inland, forests of red cedars, oaks, and hickories, and bogs of rhododendrons, occupy the hillsides.

GETTING HERE

This chapter includes sporting activities along the I-95 corridor, the highway that hugs the Connecticut coast from Greenwich to Stonington. On Sunday nights in summer, the lanes of the interstate heading toward New York City are transformed into a virtual parking lot, with cars lining up from the Connecticut coast, Newport, Cape Cod, and all other points along the eastern coast.

In the eastern half of Connecticut, smaller roads that are far more scenic head south from I-95. Route 146 connects Branford to Guilford. South of Waterford and New London, Route 213 leads to such treats as Harkness Memorial State Park and Ocean Beach Park. Route 1 from Mystic to Westerly, Rhode Island, is crowded in the summertime, but there are many side roads leading to lonely bluffs.

The Activities

ONE, IF BY LAND

Ballooning

Mystic River Balloon Adventures (17 Carriage Drive, Stonington; 203-535-0283) takes people on hot-air balloon rides over the Mystic and Stonington coastline.

Birding

Migrating shorebirds are prevalent along the Connecticut coastline in late spring and fall. Green-backed herons, yellow warblers, snowy egrets, swallows, ospreys, doves, and Canada geese are just some of the birds sighted along the tidal pools and beaches.

The Norfolk Islands contain the state's largest heron rookery as well as nesting seabirds. Contact the Connecticut Audubon Society for organized tours.

The 152-acre **Larsen Sanctuary** (2325 Main Street, Fairfield; 203-259-6305) is the main center for the Connecticut Audubon Society. The sanctuary, located off exit 44 of the Merritt Parkway, cares for injured birds, including bald eagles and peregrine falcons. The sanctuary has more than 6 miles of trails, with a diversity of habitats including nine ponds and two swamps.

The 840-acre **Connecticut Audubon Coastal Center** at Milford Point (203-878-7440; www.ctaudubon.org/centers/coastal/costal.htm) is one of the best spots in the state for birding. Of the 399 species known in Connecticut, over 300 have been recorded here. The coast is very good for shorebird and waterfowl migrations. There are nesting piping plovers, least terns, American oystercatchers (rare in the state), and both types of night herons. Ask about the naturalist-guided canoe trips to the Charles E. Wheeler State Wildlife Management Area, one of the few remaining unaltered areas on the Connecticut coast. To get to the Coastal Center, from I-95 take exit 34 to the end of the ramp, where there is a signal light. Turn left and go 0.2 mile to another light. Turn right onto Milford Point Road, and go past Naugatuck Avenue and the tennis courts. At the end of Milfort Point Road, turn right onto Seaview Road and enter.

The most surprising place to spot a hawk is **Lighthouse Point Park** in New Haven. Hawk watchers are present daily from late

August through November. It's a good place to learn about raptors. To get there when traveling eastbound on I-95, take exit 50 and go straight to the second traffic light. Turn right onto Townsend Avenue. Go 2.2 miles, and turn right onto Lighthouse Road. Go 0.7 mile to the park entrance. If you're heading westbound on I-95, take exit 51 and go 1 mile. Turn left onto Townsend Avenue and go 2.2 miles. Turn right onto Lighthouse Road and go 0.7 mile to the park entrance.

Hammonasset Beach is known for its migrating shorebirds, waders, seabirds, and wintering waterfowl and owls. The east end of the large beach, with its salt marshes, is popular with birders. Park in the lot next to Meig's Point Nature Center and see what's been written in the daily log. Head here in the early morning or late afternoon to avoid the beach crowds. Take exit 62 off I-95, then go one mile south. Jerry Connolly, president of the **Menunkatuck Audubon Society** in Madison, conducts bird walks at Hammonasset Beach State Park every Saturday in May, June, September, October, and November. The tours leave at 7:50 AM from the Audubon Shop, 871 Boston Post Road, Madison; 203-245-9056. Cost is $2.

Groton's **Bluff Point Coastal Reserve** attracts joggers, hikers, mountain bikers, and, yes, birders. The railroad tracks at the entrance are considered the state's "hot corner," where large numbers of migrating land birds can be spotted during spring and fall mornings. Take Route 117 off I-95 South. Turn right onto Route 1. After 0.3 mile turn left onto Depot Street next to the town hall. The road passes under a railroad bridge and becomes dirt. Parking is ahead.

Captain John Wadsworth takes bird lovers aboard the heated *Sunbeam Express* in January and February to view bald eagles. These majestic birds can be found hovering above the Yankee atomic power plant on the Connecticut River. **Captain John's Sport Fishing Center,** 15 First Street, Waterford, CT 06385; 860-443-7259.

Golf

Shennecosset Golf Course in Groton (203-445-0262) was designed by Donald Ross, recognized as one of the premier golf course architects of all time. He designed more than 400 courses in his lifetime, but most of these classics have been renovated. Like most Ross designs, the fairways at Shennecosset are generous, the greens small, roundish, and always sloping toward ruin. Many of the holes reward you with views of Long Island Sound.

You'll be golfing with blue herons if you golf at **Longshore Club Park** (203-222-7535), along the coast and the Saugatuck River in Westport. The winds here can wreak havoc on the average golfer and the greens can be tricky, but the setting more than makes up for it.

Nearby, the par-72 **H. Smith Richardson Golf Course** in Fairfield (203-255-6094) is one of the better municipal golf courses in the state. Locals realize that fact, so getting tee times on weekends can be tough.

Sterling Farms Golf Club in Stamford (203-329-7888) is a lush municipal course that's reasonably priced, but there may be restrictions for out-of-towners on weekends.

Horseback Riding

Windswept Farm in Stamford (203-322-4984) offers trail rides for experienced riders. North of Norwalk, **Chance Hill Equestrian Center** (203-762-3234) and **Stonyside Farms** (203-762-7984) offer trail rides in Wilton. **Greystone Farms** in North Stonington (203-535-3696) offers rides and lessons in the eastern part of the state.

Mountain Biking

Westwoods Trails, at Guilford. *Distance:* Variable. *Time:* 1 to 2 hours.

Difficulty: Easy to moderate. *Directions:* Take I-95 exit 57 to Route 1 East. After 0.5 mile, just before Bishop's Orchards, turn right on Peddlers Road. One mile later, you'll see parking on the left side of the road. Get a map at Bishop's Orchards before starting out.

Who would have known that a mere two miles from the crowded corridor of I-95 sits a 1,000-acre-plus preserve with more than 40 miles of trails crisscrossing it? You'll definitely need a map for this maze, and soon you'll be enjoying one of the largest wooded areas in coastal Connecticut. Westwoods is a mecca for the hiker or mountain biker.

Mountain bikers will want to follow the Green Square Trail west or the Orange Trail (north–south) on some technical singletrack and doubletrack runs weaving through the woods and over barren rock. Westwoods offers by far the best network of trails this close to Long Island Sound.

Bluff Point, at Groton. *Distance:* Variable. *Time:* 1 hour. *Difficulty:* Easy. *Directions:* From I-95, take exit 88 and head south on Route 117. Take a right on Route 1 and drive 0.3 mile to Depot Road. Turn left until you see the sign for Bluff Point Coastal Reserve. (See the description of Bluff Point under "Walks and Rambles," later in this chapter.)

Numerous singletrack runs spread out from the wide main trail like spokes on a wheel. Simply choose one and ramble along the shores or inland to the John Winthrop house.

You can combine your ride with a visit to nearby **Haley Farm State Park.** Once a working 17th-century farm, the site now offers rolling pasture, large stone walls, and ponds. To get there, from the junction of Routes 1 and 117, take Route 1 east for 1.1 miles. Turn right onto Route 215, and half a mile later, turn right onto Brook Street. After another half-mile, turn right onto Haley Farm Lane.

Road Biking

Traffic on Connecticut roadways can be heavy, but the state is big enough for bikers to leave the city and highways behind and find their own stretch of country road. Although Connecticut is not usually thought of as a good road biking state, the following rides will convince you otherwise.

Westport Loop. *Distance:* 25 miles (loop). *Time:* 2 to 3 hours. *Difficulty:* Easy to moderate. *Directions:* Take exit 18 off I-95 and turn left toward Route 1. At 0.4 mile on the left, there's a sign for the parking lot.

This ride takes you on the backcountry roads of Westport to Fairfield and then curves back again on arguably the most wondrous stretch of coastline in Connecticut, in Southport. Turn left out of the parking lot and make your first right onto Green Farms Road. This starts your rolling ride through a residential area. The shoulder is small here, so be wary of traffic. One mile from the start, turn left onto Hills Point Road. Slope downhill past the cattails, and the salt marsh soon gives way to the beach and waters of Long Island Sound. Compo Beach appears on your left; large homes with well-manicured gardens are on your right. This trip is a treat in early May when the tulips and forsythia are in bloom.

At 2 miles, fork right, away from the shoreline on South Compo Road's large shoulder. Continue straight along the stately maples onto Route 136 North. Cross Route 1 past the meadows of Winslow Park. Sprawling country estates now turn up on both sides of the road. The ride is relatively level, with short hills. At the 6-mile mark, turn right at the second stop sign, following Route 136 North. This part of the ride has more of a rural feel, with old stone walls, horse farms, ponds, and small creeks wherever you look—yet more and more estates are being built as suburbia creeps in.

Just past the 11th mile, turn right on Route 58 South. Beyond the tall pines and maples, Hemlock Reservoir appears on the left. Traffic starts to heat up as you head downhill into Fairfield and turn right onto North Benson Road (Route 135 South). You'll pass the campus of Fairfield University, cross under I-95, and turn right onto Old Post Road. This is the center of historic **Fairfield,** with its village green, town hall, and houses dating from 1790.

A little after the 21-mile mark, turn right onto Sasco Hill Road and then left onto Harbor Road. This will take you into the ritzy town of **Southport,** where actor Paul Newman and ex–General Electric head honcho Jack Welch have homes. A long inlet forms a picturesque harbor, more reminiscent of Camden, Maine, than the Connecticut shoreline. Sailboats in the water are with the exclusive Pequot Yacht Club.

A right turn before the dead end onto Old South Road, a left onto Pequot Avenue, and another left onto Beachside Avenue will bring you to a row of dream homes. Shortly thereafter, Green Farms Road comes in from the right. Simply take a right at the light to return to the parking lot. More appropriate would be a left turn, which brings your sweaty body to the waters of **Sherwood Island State Park.** They'll waive your bike fee.

Avid riders who happen to be in the Fairfield area should contact **The Sound Cyclist Bicycling Club** (203-840-1757). The group sponsors rides along the coast or back roads of Fairfield County on weekends and weeknights.

Route 146, Guilford to Stony Creek. *Distance:* 14 miles (round-trip). *Time:* 2 hours. *Difficulty:* Easy to moderate. *Directions:* Park on the Guilford Town Green.

From the Town Green, proceed south to Route 146 West. Heading southwest from Guilford, Route 146 is a relatively flat rural route that takes you past countless farms and saltwater marshes. Turn left on Thimble Island Road to reach the fishing village of Stony Creek. This is a good place to have lunch (try the **Stony Creek Fish Market** for deli sandwiches) and watch the boats amble in and out of the docks. Worth a visit is the **Stony Creek Puppet House Theater,** once the site of Orson Welles's Mercury Theater. When you tire of the scene (it might take a couple days), simply get back on your bikes and return on Route 146 East to Guilford.

Old Saybrook Loop. *Distance:* 7 miles (loop). *Time:* 1 hour. *Difficulty:* Easy. *Directions:* Leave your car on Main Street in Old Saybrook.

This easy loop simply goes around Route 154 in Old Saybrook, giving you a good dose of sea and sun along the way. From Main Street, turn left on College Street or Route 154. You will go through a residential area before reaching the beach. Veer right along the causeway and look at the water. This is where the Connecticut River meets Long Island Sound. At the 2-mile mark are some picnic tables and a good opportunity for photos of the harbor. From here, pass Knollwood Beach and follow the bike signs on Route 154 as you roll by salt marsh. When the road ends, turn right at the signs for Old Saybrook and you'll meet up with Main Street once again.

Connecticut River, at Essex. *Distance:* 22 miles (loop). *Time:* 3 hours. *Difficulty:* Moderate. *Directions:* Exit 3 off Route 9 will bring you to Essex Center.

Stretching 410 miles to the Canadian border, the Connecticut River is New England's longest. One of the most serene portions is from the mouth to Middletown, home to more than 50 shipyards in the mid-1800s. Sea captains who made their living from the West Indian, Chinese, and African trade lived in clapboard houses on the river's banks.

The Connecticut River as seen from the ride through Essex

The village of Deep River was once known as Ivorytown, because its major industry was the manufacture of piano keys from tons of elephant tusks.

However, by the latter half of the 19th century, the region was in a sad state of decline. The river was dammed and polluted, earning its reputation as the country's "best landscaped sewer." Spring runs of salmon and shad disappeared, and people turned their backs on the water. We can thank the Connecticut River Watershed Council for the restoration of water quality to the river and its tributaries. Shad and salmon have started to return, and wetlands and estuaries necessary for wildlife habitat have reappeared. Anglers, canoeists, sailors, birdwatchers, and bikers have followed the wildlife back to the river.

This ride starts in the center of Essex, where you take a right on North Main Street and continue on River Road. Captains' houses have been replaced by stately Colonial, Victorian, and Federal-style homes whose manicured lawns slope to the lazy river's edge. The road turns inland at Essex Street, crossing marshes inundated with migrating birds. At Route 154, turn right and continue on this fairly congested road through the towns of Deep River and Chester. Take another right on Route 82 and cross the river on what was, when it was built in 1913, one of the largest drawbridges in the world.

Sitting on the eastern bank of the Connecticut River in East Haddam is the four-story gingerbread **Goodspeed Opera House.** Opened in 1876 to present vaudeville acts and minstrel shows, the theater was restored in the 1960s and now stages revivals of Gershwin, Porter, and Rogers & Hammerstein musicals.

After a strenuous uphill climb, Route 82 levels off and veers right. Turn right at the sign for **Gillette Castle State Park** and you'll eventually see a fieldstone citadel that looks like a poor medieval prop for one of Goodspeed's plays. The actor William Gillette, who amassed millions playing Sherlock Holmes, had this castle built in 1917. Venture inside to learn a lesson or two on inferior interior decorating before strolling through the grounds (which Gillette thankfully left unscathed).

A right turn on Route 148 will have you gliding downhill past the quaint village of Hadlyme to the dock of the ferry. Pay the 75-cent fare and climb aboard with your bike to cross the Connecticut River. Continue straight until you reach Route 154, where you take a left and return to Essex.

Village Provisions (860-767-7376) in Essex rents bicycles in the summer months.

Mystic. *Distance:* 21 miles (loop). *Time:* 2 to 3 hours. *Difficulty:* Moderate. *Directions:* I-95 exit 90 will bring you to the town of Mystic.

Connecticut's coastal Route 1 from Mystic to Stoningham is one large parking lot in the summertime. Avoid the traffic and head to the hills on this trail that hugs the Mystic harbor before traveling through rarely seen Connecticut pastures.

Start in the center of Mystic, cross the drawbridge by foot, and take your first right on Gravel Street. A left on Eldredge and a right on Pearl will take you through Mystic's historic housing district, dating from the 1850s, the height of the whaling industry. Across the harbor is a lighthouse where a schooner is usually docked.

Head right on River Road, where you'll find ospreys nesting atop poles, and numerous geese, ducks, and swans lounging on the Mystic River. You'll glide along the river, coasting under I-95 and crossing Route 27 before going straight on North Stonington Road. Veer left on Lantern Hill Road to swing past expansive farmland dotted with secluded ponds. A right on Route 214 will bring you straight to the **Foxwoods Casino.** I bet you've never biked to a casino before, but if you're dreaming of that new $3,700 Trek Y-33 with Fox air/oil rear shock and Rockshox Judy SL suspension forks, then lock up, run to the blackjack tables, and just say "Hit me!"

From here, take a right on Route 2, which is heavily congested but has a large shoulder. You'll soon turn right on Route 201 South past silos and the wholesome smell of manure. The salt of the sea will seem like a distant memory with every whiff. At Route 184, go straight onto North Stonington Road past the Old Mystic fire station (don't turn left onto Route 27). This will get you back safe and sound to River Road and the fried clam rolls at Sea Swirl in Mystic.

A good place to rent bikes in Mystic is the **Mystic Cycle Center,** on Route 1, just outside of Mystic toward Stonington; 860-572-7433.

Walks and Rambles

Connecticut's extensive network of blue-blazed hiking trails weave across relatively flat terrain, creating one of the best walking systems in the Northeast. The trails are all inland, through forests of maples, oaks, and birches. However, there are several coastal walks not associated with the blue blazes that are worthy of a visit. **Connecticut Forest and Park Association** (16 Meriden Road, Rockfall, CT 06481-2691; 860-346-TREE) has information on the blue-blazed trails and hosts a trails day in early summer to introduce more walkers to the system. The association also publishes *The Connecticut Walk Book,* which details all the walks.

Nature Center for Environmental Activities, at Westport. *Distance:* Variable. *Time:* 30 to 60 minutes. *Difficulty:* Easy. *Directions:* In Westport, at 10 Woodside Lane; 203-227-7253.

Driving past the multimillion-dollar estates tucked behind the stone walls of Westport, you finally reach this divine spit of land left undeveloped in suburbia. Sixty-two acres of deciduous forest, open fields, and swamp area line more than 2 miles of walking trails. A good introductory walk is on the Swamp Loop. Butterflies whiz by and birds greet you on the soft trail, a welcome respite from the hum of autos on I-95 or the bustling crowds at nearby Sherwood Island State Park. Passing through a section of old stately elms, don't be surprised to see wild turkeys wandering the grounds. Along with deer, pheasants, and the occasional fox, the turkeys call this home. The trail is covered with wood chips where you make your way through swamp habitat back to the parking lot. A good trail for young children.

Connecticut Audubon Center, at Fairfield. *Distance:* Variable. *Time:* 30 to 60 minutes. *Difficulty:* Easy. *Directions:* In Fairfield, at 2325 Burr Street; 203-259-6305.

This 160-acre preserve in the north end of Fairfield is lined with 6 miles of trails through marshes, meadows, and a pine forest. With small signs that tell which tree is the white oak or the Norwegian spruce, the network of paths is ideal for children. Butterflies in the meadows and large frogs in the pond enhance the experience.

Westwoods Trails, at Guilford. *Distance:* Variable. *Time:* 1 to 2 hours. *Difficulty:* Easy to moderate. *Directions:* Take I-95 exit 57 to Route 1 East. After 0.5 mile, just before Bishop's Orchards, turn right on Peddlers Road. One mile later, you'll see parking on the left side of the road. Get a map at Bishop's Orchards.

There are more than 40 miles of paths in this 1,000-acre-plus preserve over swamps, streams, and granite outcroppings, all deep in the forest. Hikers can take the White Circle Trail, which starts on planks over a marsh of ferns and buttercups before rising on a series of rock ledges deep into the forest. You can hook up with the Green Square and Green Circle Trails, then cross a small creek and head back up into the hills before meeting up with the White Circle Trail once again for the route back to the car.

Salt Meadow National Wildlife Refuge, at Westbrook. *Distance:* Variable. *Time:* 30 to 60 minutes. *Difficulty:* Easy. *Directions:* From Route 1 in Clinton, turn left on Route 145 North and follow Old Clinton Road for 3 miles.

This 192-acre wilderness area has close to 3 miles of trails that meander through salt marsh, shrubland, and woodland. It's a fine spot for bird-watching, especially in the spring when warblers pass through.

Glacial Park, near Groton. *Distance:* 0.75 mile. *Time:* 45 minutes. *Difficulty:* Easy to moderate. *Directions:* From Groton, take Route 117 North to Sandy Hollow Road. Take a left and then another left onto Whalehead Road. The sign for Glacial Park Boulder Train Site will be on your right. There is a small parking spot across the street.

Unless you enjoy boulder hopping, the walk through the bizarre terrain at Glacial Park is one that you'll probably try just once. Cross the street and enter the forest under the power lines. About 300 yards later, the trail splits. The main trail veers left while the alternate trail forks to the right. If you are in any condition to rock jump, I highly suggest the main trail.

The path proceeds up a small hill where you suddenly see hundreds of boulders in a ravine to your right. Your first thought is that some construction worker has played a practical joke on you with his lift. The truth is that these boulders are remains of a moraine from the Wisconsin glacier, which passed through 12,000 years ago. This huge rock collection is a result of glacial melting. In several moments, you'll be clambering over these massive stones, trying to find the blotches of blue paint that somehow denote a trail. Don't worry, the torture will end in about 15 minutes when the main trail catches up with the alternate trail and loops back to the parking lot. Try to keep a sense of direction, because the path has arrows pointed every which way but the exit.

Harkness Memorial State Park, at Waterford. *Distance:* Variable. *Time:* 1 hour. *Difficulty:* Easy. *Directions:* From Route 156, turn right on Route 213 and follow the signs to the park.

A problem with most of the Connecticut coast is its easy accessibility. Interstate 95 skirts the shore, bringing far too many people to the same outdoor spot you cherish. Near East Lyme and Waterford, however, I-95 heads a wee bit north, so people have to make that extra effort to get to the water. This is where you find gems like the 234-acre Harkness Memorial State Park. Bequeathed to the state in 1952, the park with its 42-room Italianate mansion, manicured lawns, and gardens is a perfect place for a stroll or picnic. Tour the house and then head outside on small stony paths that snake through the gardens. In May, this is quite a treat, with many of the perennials in bloom. The great expanse of lawn slopes down to the shore. Swimming is prohibited (head to nearby Ocean Beach in New London) but you're free to bring your pole and surf-cast for stripers and blues. In the summer, a concert series brings well-known performers to the grounds. Call 860-442-9199 for a list of performers.

Bluff Point Coastal Reserve, at Groton. *Distance:* 4.5 miles (round-trip). *Time:* 2 hours. *Difficulty:* Easy. *Directions.* From I-95, take exit 88 and head south on Route 117 until you meet the intersection of Route 1 in Groton. Take a right onto Route 1 and drive 0.3 mile to Depot Road. Turn left and continue until you see the sign for Bluff Point.

Bluff Point offers one of Connecticut's few coastal walks that's not on sand. Far from campsites and crowded beaches, this 778-acre state park in Groton is one of the most undeveloped areas of the Connecticut coastline. Hikers have to contend with horseback riders and mountain bikers, but they usually stay off the main trail. Keep to the wide dirt path or you might end up on one of the bike trails.

Stay to the right, and the trail winds along the Poquonock River before heading inland and reaching the bluffs. From here you can see directly across Long Island Sound to New York's Fishers Island. To the left is Rhode Island's Watch Hill. If time allows, meander among Bluff Point's beach plums, beach peas, and white shore roses to Bushy Point. Then turn around and follow the main trail as it curves inland. You'll pass the site of Governor Fitz-John Winthrop's farmhouse, built in the early 1700s, where it's believed the governor had a brick chimney the size of a bedroom in his basement to hide from Indian attacks. When the inland trail ends, head right to return to the parking lot.

TWO, IF BY SEA

Canoeing

East River, at Guilford. *Distance:* 4–6 miles (round-trip). *Time:* As long as you need. *Difficulty:* Easy. *Directions:* Take exit 59 off I-95 and follow signs to Route 1 East. Drive 2.1 miles on Route 1 and turn right onto Neck Road. Bear right a few hundred yards later and follow the boat launching signs. There is plenty of parking at the Guilford Harbor boat launch.

It's a rarity to find decent canoeing along the coast, but the East River, which borders the towns of Guilford and Madison, offers one of those unique opportunities. Extending 5 miles from Long Island Sound inland, the narrow winding river weaves through salt marshes before reaching high ground. If you time your paddle right, you can canoe upstream with the tide coming in and back with the tide coming out, so you're with the current the whole trip.

About 1.5 miles from put-in at Guilford Harbor, you'll pass under the first of many bridges, this one being for Amtrak. In the early stages of your paddling, you'll probably spot herons and egrets hunting for small fish and crabs. But as you get farther and farther from the Sound, canoeing under Route 1 and I-95, you might see osprey and marsh hawks circling above a forest of oak, sassafras, and cedar. When the hum of I-95 fades away, drop your line for flukes, stripers, and blues, and whisk away the day.

Fishing

There's a reason why the popularity of saltwater fly fishing has outpaced all other categories of sportfishing in New England for the past several years. It's called striped bass. Found all along the New England coast, these fish have voracious appetites, grow to more than 50 pounds, and fight like champions. Striped bass can be found in remarkable numbers along the Connecticut coast from Greenwich to Stonington. If you find yourself on the beach when stripers are around, be prepared for some of the best fishing on the East Coast.

Starting in mid-May, stripers arrive in Long Island Sound from their winter home near Chesapeake Bay. These early arrivals are a bit on the small side, weighing about 5 pounds, and are nicknamed schoolies. The bigger stripers prefer 54-degree water temperatures, and they arrive in force by late June. They begin to fill their hungry bellies with schools of herring, sand eels, cinder worms, and (fortunately for anglers) artificial flies.

There's a misconception that you have to throw your line way out there to catch these suckers, but actually many stripers are snatched within the length of your rod. If you are on a beach with some breaking waves lapping at your feet, the stripers will most often be feeding right in the whitewash. Indeed, if you've ever gone swimming in the surf, you've probably noticed the small drop-off where the waves break near the beach. Stripers like to pin sand eels and other prey against this ledge while feeding in the surf. If you can position yourself about a dozen feet or so away from that ledge and cast beyond it, you're in for some fine striper fishing.

Along the Atlantic coast, stripers and blues can be hooked in late spring and summer. In Connecticut, they can be found anywhere on the coast from the base of Holyoke Dam on the Connecticut River to Bluff Point Coastal Reserve in Groton. Individual anglers are permitted to take two striped bass per day. Only one of these fish can measure between 24 and 32 inches; the other fish must be 41 inches or longer. On party boats or charters, however, two fish 28 inches or longer may be taken per day.

But don't just settle for stripers or blues. Every year from the middle of June well into October, ocean fluke fishing on the Sound comes into full swing. They usually follow the schools of squid and sand eels that migrate along the 20- to 70-foot South Shore depths. The fluke move inshore from the Continental Shelf in April and early May and feed throughout the spring and summer until it's time for them to head offshore again in the fall.

If you plan on surf-casting, simply go to the yellow pages and find the local bait and tackle shop. Once you purchase some flies, the folks at the shop are usually willing to ante up their secret hideaways, especially if they know you're from out of town and won't be back bullying in on their precious fish. Or opt for a charter boat that takes anglers out on one- to six-person boats in search of stripers, blues, cod, pollock, flukes, porgies, and flounder. The cost for a six-person charter runs about $800 per day. This might seem high, but $125 or so per person is a small price to pay when you're out with your friends all day hooking stripers.

There are numerous charters to choose from. Here's a handful that come recommended: *Miss Nora* in South Norwalk (203-866-9671), *Catch 'Em* in Westbrook (860-223-1876; www.catchemcharters.com), *Carol Marie* in Bridgeport (203-264-2891), **Captain John's Sunbeam Fleet** in Waterford (860-443-7259; www.sunbeamfleet.com), *Magic* in Noank (860-455-9942), and *Benmar* in Mystic (860-521-3168; www.happycaptain.com). **Shaffer's Boat Livery** (860-536-8713) rents 16-foot skiffs so you can play the role of captain ($70 a day). For a complete listing of captains and their boats, contact the **Connecticut State Tourism Office** and ask for the *Connecticut Vacation Guide;* call 1-800-282-6863 or visit www.ctbound.org.

Sailing

With relatively little surf, good prevailing winds, and numerous island anchorages, the Long Island Sound shore is an excellent place to learn how to sail. The **Sound Sailing School** in Norwalk (203-838-1110), adjacent to Calf Pasture Beach, offers instruction and also rents everything from Daysailors to J-44s. Close to the Norwalk Islands, this is a great location for a day or overnight charter. Close by, the **Norwalk Sailing School** (203-852-1857) also rents sailboats and offers instruction.

Tired of the male-dominated sailing world, Sherry Jagerson founded **Women's Sailing Adventures** (39 Woodside Avenue, Westport; 203-227-7413) in 1989 to teach women the fine art of sailing. An inveterate sailor and impassioned instructor, Jagerson offers two-, three-, and seven day courses out of Westport on 37- to 44-foot boats. She also arranges a four-hour beginners course on J-24s; more than three-quarters of the class time is conducted under sail, and the student-to-instructor ratio is two or three to one.

Longshore Sailing School in Westport (203-226-4646; www.long shoresailingschool.com) is one of the most popular day-sailing schools in the country, especially for children ages 9 to 16. Twelve hours of instruction in four sessions over two weekends are provided for all levels, at the mouth of the saltwater Saugatuck River on boats under 16 feet long. Among the essential skills taught are how to rig a boat and how to start, stop, trim the sail, jibe, and tack.

For instruction in the eastern part of the state, contact **Coastline Sailing School** (8 Marsh Road, Eldridge Yard, Noank; 203-536-2689). Lessons are available for all levels of experience.

Sterling Yacht Charters (44 Water Street, Mystic; 203-572-1111) offers customized bareboat and skippered charters along the Connecticut coast. Rental times range from an afternoon to a month depending on the size of boat and number of passengers.

Scuba Diving

Rex Dive Center in South Norwalk (203-853-4148; www.rexdivecenter.com) offers wreck diving in the Sound or good night diving to see nocturnal lobster crawling on the ocean floor. The center also features PADI certification for advanced open water and drysuit diving.

Sea Kayaking

The Small Boat Shop in South Norwalk (203-854-5223; www.the smallboatshop.com) offers one-day guided sea kayaking tours of the Norwalk Islands. Starting at the shop's dock on the Norwalk River, you paddle past Manresa Point and across the channel to Sheffield Island to see its historic lighthouse. After lunch at Shea Island, the journey continues to Chimon Island, site of a national wildlife preserve. Herons, snowy egrets, American oystercatchers, and ospreys have been spotted on the shores. Cost of the trip is $90; instructional tours are offered for $110.

Southeast of Branford, the picturesque fishing harbor of Stony Creek is the gateway to a group of 32 inhabited islands known as the Thimble Islands. An apt name, some of these islands are just large enough to hold one house, as if they were nothing more than houseboats at their moorings. Others have longs stretches of untrammeled beach, ideal for small boat travel. **Stony Creek Kayak** (203-481-6401; www.stonycreekkayak.com) features guided half-day, full-day, sunset, and even full-moon paddles around the Thimbles. Expect to hear the lore of Captain Kidd's hidden treasure on Money Island (no one has ever found it). Also listen for the tale of Tom Thumb's courtship of a diminutive gal on Cut-in-Two Island. P. T. Barnum broke off the romance and had Tom marry another of his circus midgets. Bare Island was once a granite quarry. Indeed, Stony Creek granite can be found in such famous structures as the Lincoln Memorial and the Brooklyn Bridge. Come have a look at a leisurely pace.

For those with their own sea kayak, the trip from Old Lyme to

Great Island is arguably the best paddle on the Connecticut coast. The island is situated at the mouth of the Connecticut River, and you wind through a small channel on the eastern side of the island before retracing your strokes back to the put-in.

Mystic River Rentals (860-536-8381) features guided tours on the Mystic River for groups of five or more.

Wind Surfing

Darien Windsurfing on Weed Beach near Darien (203-852-1857) features one-week courses during the summer.

In South Norwalk, **Gone With the Wind Surfing** (203-852-1857) rents sailboards and offers instruction on Calf Pasture Beach. Spectators are welcome to check out their wind surfing races, every Wednesday at 6 PM.

Longshore Sailing School in Westport (203-226-4646; www.long shoresailingschool.com) offers wind surfing instruction.

A DAY AT THE BEACH

There's no just reason for Connecticut beaches to be so prohibitive in cost. Sure, you're welcome to head to Greenwich Point Park in the off-season. But come mid-May, this park and many of the other town beaches along the Connecticut shore are off-limits to out-of-towners. Other beaches like Compo Beach in Westport charge a ludicrous $30 per day for nonresidents. Fortunately, the finest stretches of sand along the Connecticut shore, Hammonasset and Rocky Neck, are state parks open to all.

Why the need for affluent towns to feel so privileged? It's not as if these spits of sand are exquisitely beautiful, like the white rolling dunes of Province Lands or Nauset Beach on Cape Cod or the rugged shoreline Winslow Homer made famous on the Maine shore. The Connecticut beaches for the most part are narrow widths of hard-packed bronze sand that slopes gently to water that has very little surf. They are ideal for young families because of the long, gradual slope and shallow water. People who yearn to ride the waves often make the trek east to the beaches of Rhode Island.

For New Yorkers who need to cool off, **Sherwood Island State Park** in Westport is the closest Connecticut state beach park to the Big Apple. It's a good 75-minute drive from Manhattan to get here, and the beach is not nearly as big or white as Jones Beach or Robert Moses Beach on Long Island—and I-95 in Connecticut can be just as crowded as the Long Island Expressway on a hot summer day. The 2-mile-long stretch of sand is wide and flat, ideal for children. There are two large picnic groves with wooden tables and trees for welcome shade. To reach Sherwood Island, take I-95 North to exit 18 and turn right onto the Sherwood Island Connector. Cost is $8 per car.

There are also places to stop before Westport where it's possible to hit the beach. East of Greenwich, Stamford's **Cove Island Park** is an 83-acre green space on the Sound. It's a popular spot to jog or in-line skate on a paved trail or to walk on the green grass under willow trees and watch the fishing boats heading out in the early morning hours. Part of the shore is rocky, but it leads to a nice crescent beach at the point bordered by two rock jetties. Take exit 8 off I-95 and follow Elm Street, turning left on Cove Street. In season, only residents can park in the lot, but it's an easy walk of four or five blocks to Cove Island if you must park elsewhere.

Norwalk's **Calf Pasture Beach** is a long, sweeping beach that looks out onto the Norwalk Islands and a lighthouse. A boardwalk and a new playground line the beach. Take exit 16 off I-95 to East Avenue and then to Gregory Boulevard. Cost of parking is $15.

The sand at Westport's **Compo Beach** seems a little whiter, a little more pristine than on most Connecticut beaches. The long, sweeping beach has its fair share of seashells. It has an excellent wooden playground with small turrets and tunnels for kids to roam in. Take exit 17 from I-95, head east across the Saugatuck River, and turn right (south) on Compo Road. Weekday parking is $15, weekend parking is $30.

Rickers, Penfield, and Jennings Beaches are Fairfield's contingent of beaches. It's basically the same stretch of sand interspersed with private property. Rickers is off-limits to nonresidents. Of the remaining two, Jennings has the largest parking lot and thus provides the best chance of getting in. Jennings also features a modern playground for kids. Cost of parking is $12 weekdays, $20 weekends, or you can opt for the $75 nonresident summer fee.

One of the least-known state park beaches is **Silver Sands Beach,** in Milford. Connected to the town's Walnut Beach, Silver Sands has a long boardwalk from the parking lot across a marsh (good for birdwatching, but not great if you're carrying food and sand toys). The beach is small compared with other state park beaches like Hammonasset or Sherwood Island, but alas is less well known. Take exit 34 off I-95 to Route 1 East and turn right on Pumpkin Delight to the coast. No fee.

New Haven's **Lighthouse Point Park** was once the popular last stop on the trolley line. On any given Sunday in the 1920s, you might find baseball greats Babe Ruth or Ty Cobb playing a makeshift game for their fans. Today, the only feature remaining from these times is the Lighthouse Point carousel, whose shiny brass poles and galloping horses look like they were built only yesterday. The carousel is housed in a historic building next to a lighthouse. The long, rouge-colored beach is popular with locals in the summer. In the fall, birders make the pilgrimage here to see migrating hawks and other raptors. Take exit 50 (northbound) or exit 51 (southbound) off I-95 and follow Townsend Avenue down to Lighthouse Road (follow the signs). Cost to enter the park is $6 for nonresidents.

Connecticut's longest stretch of public sand is in Madison at **Hammonasset Beach.** The 2-mile-long beach is narrow, not more than 15 yards, so it can be crammed with bodies on summer days. But the sand is soft and the water is cool. There's a long boardwalk for walking or in-line skating past the sun worshipers, a large grassy area for picnicking, and a good rock jetty for trying your luck at hooking stripers. The Meig's Point Nature Center (203-245-8743) arranges bird-watching walks, bike rides, canoe trips, and nature workshops for all ages. Also here is the largest campground on the coast (see "Camping"). Take exit 62 off I-95. Cost to enter the park for nonresidents is $8 weekdays, $12 weekends.

Turn right on Waterside Lane in Clinton to reach the **Town Beach.** This peaceful small beach is idyllic for small children or for couples who want to relax on the swing chair and watch the boats head in and out of the nearby harbor. The small inlet is not nearly as open to the wrath of the Sound as nearby Hammonasset. There's also a small playground. Cost of parking is $7 for nonresidents.

The sweeping white sand beach of **Rocky Neck State Park,** near South Lyme, is a mile long, but like Hammonasset isn't very wide. Yet the rising bluffs and crescent shape make this one of the prettiest beaches on the Connecticut coast. The only distraction is the Amtrak train running by every hour. The park offers nature walks along Bride Brook and Four Mile River. More than likely, you'll have the paths to yourself—a pleasant getaway from the wall-to-wall beach towels carpeting the sand. Birdwatchers have sighted cormorants, snowy egrets, and kingfishers on the trails. Take exit 72 off I-95 to reach the park. Cost to enter the park for nonresidents is $6 weekdays, $10 weekends.

It's hard to get bored at New London's **Ocean Beach Park.** Not only does it offer one of the nicest beaches on the shore—a half-mile-long stretch of sand that's significantly wider than Hammonasset or Rocky Neck—but the park also features three 50-foot-high water slides, a wide wooden boardwalk down the length of the beach, a miniature golf course, an arcade, and lots of food options, plus a large new playground. Take Route 213 to Ocean Avenue and head south. Fee: $6 weekdays, $10 weekends.

In the seaside village of Noank, **Esker Point Beach** juts out on a small spit of sand, with good views of Mouse Island. The shallow swimming area is a favorite for young families, but the water level might be too low for older children. There's also a concession stand. The beach is located on Marsh Road, before crossing over to Groton's Long Point. Cost of parking is $1.

Strolling down Water Street in Stonington is like walking onto a movie set depicting America during the Revolutionary War. You'll see a row of 17th- and 18th-century houses clustered together as you make your way past the Old Lighthouse Museum to Stonington Point. **DuBois Beach** sits at the foot of Water Street, exposed to the wind and all the boats going in and out of the harbor. The shell-strewn beach and shallow waters attract families. Charge is $3 per person or $6 for a family.

CAMPGROUNDS

Many of Connecticut's state parks and forests have campgrounds. For reservations and a listing of camping facilities, contact the **Office of State Parks and Recreation,** 79 Elm Street, Hartford, CT 06106-5127; 860-424-3200.

Hammonasset Beach State Park, in Madison (203-245-1817). From the junction of Route 79 and Route 1, head 3 miles east on Route 1. There are 558 sites (none with hook-ups), flush toilets, showers, public phone, tables, and a small concession. This is the largest camping facility in Connecticut, and the beach says it all. The campground is often crowded and lacking privacy, but for beachfront property starting at $12 a night, who can complain.

Riverdale Farm Campsites, north of Clinton (860-536-4044). Take exit 62 off I-95 and drive north 200 feet to Duck Hole Road. Head east for 0.5 mile on this road, turn left over the bridge, and then left again on River Road. The camp is 1.5 miles ahead on the left. The camp provides 250 sites for RVs (100 with full hook-ups and 150 with water and electricity), flush toilets, hot showers, and a store. If you can't get into Hammonasset or just value your privacy, try this clean site. There's a spring-fed pond for swimming, and the Hammonasset River is close by for fishing.

Rocky Neck State Park, at Niantic (860-739-5471). From the junction of Route 161 and Route 156 in Niantic, head 3 miles west on Route 156. The park has 169 sites (none with hook-ups), hot showers, flush toilets, a public phone, picnic tables, and fire rings. Situated next to the mile-long Rocky Neck Beach, you can spend the day at the beach, and the early evening fishing for your dinner.

The Island, just north of Old Lyme (860-739-8316). Take exit 74 off I-95 in Lyme and head north on Route 161. Turn left on Route 1 West for 1 mile and turn right on Islanda Court. The road ends on the island. You'll find 35 sites for tent trailers or RVs (with water and electrical hook-ups) hot showers, and flush toilets. This prime locale is a small island on Lake Pattagansett. Many of the sites overlook the lake or are shaded. Lounge on the beach or go fishing.

Seaport Campgrounds, just north of Mystic (860-624-4044). Take exit 90 off I-95 and head 1.25 miles north on Route 27. Turn right on Route 184 and go another half-mile. Seaport Campgrounds is on your left. The facility features 130 sites (most with water and electrical hook-ups), picnic tables, a swimming pool, a miniature golf course, a bathhouse, a fishing pond, and a store whose wares include firewood and ice. This campground is set in a meadow with spacious sites.

Highland Orchards Resort Park, at North Stonington (1-800-624-0829). Take exit 92 off I-95 and head north on Route 49. Highland Orchards is the first driveway on the right. The park has 260 sites, picnic tables, fireplaces, hot showers, a swimming pool, sports courts, a fishing pond, and a store that sells a variety of items including ice and firewood. Sites here don't have much privacy, but the manicured lawns and century-old maple trees on this former farm property make up for it. With all the sports, the swimming pool, and organized theme dinners, this is a good spot for families.

CHAPTER TWO
Rhode Island

▶ Because Rhode Island is less than 40 miles wide, most people under-estimate the more than 400 miles of coastline in the state. The coast of the Ocean State is a complex combination of bays, estuaries, islands, sounds, and vast beaches. Salt marshes and tall, coarse reeds guard the entrance to long crescents of sand, dunes rise and fall, rocky promontories coated with lichen form an impenetrable barrier, and bluffs plunge to the waters below. This is the scenery that has enchant-ed travelers for centuries.

Most people associate Rhode Island with the palatial estates that sit on the southern end of Aquidneck Island in a town called Newport. In the late 1700s, Newport was a summer resort for wealthy planters fleeing the humidity of South Carolina, Jamaica, and Antigua. In 1783, George Washington sent his ailing nephew here to regain his strength. During the summers of the mid-1800s, Rhode Island was home to a long list of luminaries including Edgar Allen Poe, Henry Wadsworth Longfellow, George Bancroft, Robert Louis Stevenson, and John Singer Sargent.

Then came the arrival of The Four Hundred. Samuel Ward McAl-lister, friend and confidant to Mrs. William Astor, coined this name in reference to the four hundred wealthiest families in New York worth knowing. McAllister had just bought a summer home in Newport and persuaded Mrs. Astor to build a summer "cottage" there as well. The others soon followed. These so-called cottages were 50- to 70-room mansions with large stables, spacious lawns, gardens, and greenhouses—immense palaces of marble, limestone, and granite. Some of these lofty establishments, like Cornelius Vanderbilt's The Breakers, built between 1892 and 1895, and Oliver Hazard Perry Belmont's Belcourt, constructed in 1894, cost well over $5 million.

This excessive show of wealth had its share of detractors. More reserved members of the upper class spent their summers on Block Island, Jamestown, and Watch Hill. Many Washington socialites preferred Narragansett to Newport. However, the affluent were not the only ones arriving on the shores of Rhode Island. The middle class stayed at large hotels or the rows of cottages that were beginning to open up on the coast. Those who could not afford a night's accommodation made a day visit to one of the numerous amusement parks.

When the stock market crashed in 1929, many of Newport's mansions were boarded up, torn down, sold for taxes, or destroyed by vandals and fire. The resorts became vacant and the amusement parks closed. This situation lasted for only a short time. Sailors, saltwater anglers, walkers, bikers, and hordes of other travelers soon came back, and not just to Newport, but to the entire Rhode Island coast, including Block Island. Like the waves that continuously crash on the shores only to fall gently back to sea, people who have the good fortune to visit Rhode Island return with regularity.

THE TERRAIN

Look at a map of southern New England and you'll notice the large indentation known as Narragansett Bay. The same ice sheet that caused the formation of Cape Cod brought about the jagged shoreline of Rhode Island. Rock debris accumulated at the melting ice front to form a terminal moraine, an irregularly shaped ridge that fringed the lobes of ice. Over the years, the bedrock eroded. The sea stretched far north into the lowlands, creating Narragansett Basin and long, narrow Prudence and Conanicut Islands. Geologists say the soft bedrock forming the ridge of the basin is the same age as the Pennsylvania coal formations, and indeed, coal has been found at several spots within the bay.

Other areas of the coastline were created when the ice retreated. Rocks that had been carried hundreds of miles by the glacier were discarded at random as glacial erratics as the ice withdrew. This is how Watch Hill, Rhode Island's westernmost point, was formed. A glacial dumping ground, Watch Hill is a mass of large boulders, knobs, and vertiginous ridges.

GETTING HERE

Although Rhode Island is less than 40 miles wide from east to west and 50 miles long from north to south, distances between points are a lot longer than you would expect. This is due to the bizarre shape of the shoreline. From Providence to Westerly, Rhode Island, is only 53 easy miles on I-95, but reaching the central shoreline and islands is more complicated. Newport is reached via Routes 24 and 114 from the northeast, or across Newport Bridge and Route 138 from the west. To reach Narragansett from Providence, take I-95 south and switch to Routes 4 and 1. The closest ferry to Block Island departs from Galilee, just south of Narragansett. Route 1A from Narragansett north to Wickford is a scenic drive that hugs the western shores of the bay. Route 138 over the Jamestown Bridge to Conanicut Island is another picturesque journey.

The Activities

ONE, IF BY LAND

Ballooning

For one-hour balloon flights along the coast followed by a glass of champagne, contact **Kingston Balloon Company** (401-783-9386).

Birding

With more than 300 recorded species of birds, Rhode Island birding is first-rate. This is especially true of Block Island, located on the Atlantic Flyway. A colorful variety of warblers are seen on the island in early October. The **Block Island Refuge** consists of 46 acres of sandy beaches and rolling dunes. Regular ferry service is available from the Port of Galilee, south of Narragansett.

The **Norman Bird Sanctuary** in Middletown (401-846-2577) constitutes the largest area of preserved open space in Newport County. This wildlife refuge encompassing over 450 acres has 7 miles of trails that wind through a diversity of habitats. Nearly 30 acres are maintained as hay fields. Woodlands are the most prominent plant community, while four ridges provide spectacular views of the surrounding ocean and ponds. In early spring, you can find buffleheads, ruddys, glossy ibis, northern pintails, green-winged teals, goldeneyes, mergansers, and loons on the big ponds. The visitor center is situated in a 19th-century barn. *Directions:* From points north, take Route 24 South to exit 1 (Newport Beaches), and bear right off the exit, following Route 138 South through Portsmouth (approximately 7 miles). Once you pass Rhode Island Nurseries on the right, take a left onto Route 138A at the second set of traffic lights. Follow Route 138A to the first intersection and turn left onto Green End Avenue for 1.5 miles to a four-way stop. Take a right onto Third Beach Road. The sanctuary is three-quarters of a mile farther on the right.

Nearby, in Middletown, the 242-acre **Sachuest Point National Wildlife Refuge** (401-847-5511) comprises a range of habitats including saltwater and freshwater marshes, shrubland, grassland, and sandy beaches and dunes. A 3-mile trail system winds through the upland areas and along the rocky shore. More than 200 bird species seasonally inhabit the refuge, including many songbirds, ducks, and raptors. In winter, it's a great spot for ducks, loons, and grebes. *Directions:* From Route 138, travel east on Miantonomi Avenue for 0.6 mile. Continue east onto Green End Avenue for 1.2 miles, then turn right onto Paradise Avenue. Travel 1.3 miles and turn left onto Hanging Rock Road. Continue 0.3 mile, then bear right onto Sachuest Point Road and follow it to the refuge entrance.

Trustom Pond National Wildlife Refuge in South Kingston (401-364-9124) features 3 miles of walking trails through open fields and former pasture that lead to a small pond. Wood ducks, bluebirds, purple martins, and ospreys are a sampling of the more than 40 species of birds found here. *Directions:* Take Route 1 in South Kingstown to Moonstone Beach Road. Follow that road 1 mile and turn right on Matunuck Schoolhouse Road. The entrance is 0.7 mile on the left.

Ospreys sitting atop poles, and herons nesting in the marsh, can be seen by walkers and bikers visiting the 3,000-acre **Great Swamp Management Area** in West Kingston (401-222-1267). A 5.5-mile loop rings the dense woodlands of red maple, white cedar, holly, and rhododendron. (Also see "Mountain Biking.") *Directions:* Take Route 138 to the village of West Kingston and turn west onto Liberty Lane. Follow the road just under a mile until it ends at a railroad track. Then go left onto a gravel lane for about 1 mile, passing office and maintenance buildings, to the parking lot.

Bird peepers head to **Ninigret Conservation Area** (401-364-9124) in March and April to see grebes, loons, and mergansers bobbing on the waves. Even farther offshore are seals. Also visit the trails at **Ninigret National Wildlife Refuge.** *Directions:* Both sites are accessible via Route 1, just east of Route 216. Follow East Beach Road until it ends at the shore and then go left onto a gravel road. You'll see the conservation area sign and parking lot.

The **Audubon Society of Rhode Island** (401-949-5454) offers guided walks to many sites.

Golf

Rhode Island's limited public golf course offerings do have a few gems in the rough. **Triggs Memorial Golf Course** in Providence (1533 Chalkstone Avenue; 401-521-8460) is another challenging Donald Ross design dating from 1927. Expect long fairways and undulating greens. The **North Kingstown Municipal Golf Course** (Callahan Road; 401-294-0684) is sandwiched between the ocean and a Navy air base, making for some interesting play. It has a great seaside links layout on Narragansett Bay. Close by, the **Exeter Country Club** (Ten Rod Road; 401-295-8212), open to the public, has a scenic layout featuring a covered bridge.

Horseback Riding

The old-wealth families of Newport certainly had their fair share of horses back in their heyday. Even today, hoofing it on a beach near the Bellevue mansions has a certain Gatsbyesque appeal. **Newport Equestrian Center** (287 Third Beach Road, Middletown; 401-848-5440) has rides on the beach or inland for all levels of experience. On the other side of the Sakonnet River, in the farming community of Tiverton, try the **Roseland Acres Equestrian Center** (594 East

Road; 401-624-8866). **Rustic Rides Farm** in Block Island (401-466-5060) also offers instruction and trail rides, including paths along the beach.

Mountain Biking

Although it's not especially known for its off-road bike trails, Rhode Island does have three spots that are highly recommended.

Arcadia Management Area, at Arcadia. *Distance:* Varies depending on route. *Time:* 2 to 3 hours. *Difficulty:* Easy to moderate. *Directions:* Take I-95 to exit 5A onto Route 102 South. Turn right onto Route 3 South and right again, at the blinking light, onto Route 165 West. Then, 2.5 miles later, you will see a small white church on the right where you can park. For a good map, contact the Department of Environmental Management, Division of Parks and Recreation, at 401-539-2356.

Rhode Island's largest public land, the 13,817-acre Arcadia Management Area is a mecca for the state's mountain bikers. More than 30 miles of singletrack trails and less technical doubletracks and dirt roads weave through the woods.

Ride left from the church and head uphill for 0.3 mile onto Route 165. Two more lefts at a dirt road and a fork will bring you to a rocky singletrack that will test your skills almost immediately. When you reach the first set of doubletracks, you might be content to turn right under a forest of oaks and hickories. A sharp left and you'll be at the shores of Breakheart Pond. After crossing a small bridge and bearing right, more singletracks await on the left-hand side. Choose one of these trails and zip through the trees to reach Frosty Hollow Road. A left turn on this gravel road brings you directly back to your car. What a stroke of luck.

Great Swamp Management Area, near West Kingston. *Distance:* 5.5

miles (loop). *Time:* 1 hour. *Difficulty:* Easy. *Directions:* Take exit 3A off I-95 onto Route 138 East toward Kingston and Newport. Just before the junction with Route 110, turn right on Liberty Lane. Follow the road past the park buildings to the end, where there's a small parking lot and barred gateway.

Who says you can't go mountain biking and bird-watching at the same time? Certainly not the folks who run the Great Swamp Management Area, where an easy loop on grassy roads and doubletracks surrounds a wetland that is teeming with incredible bird life.

Binoculars dangling from your neck, veer left twice through the holly trees, and you'll soon arrive at a popular fishing spot, Worden Pond. Then head back, turning left on the main trail to a large dike and marsh. A glossy ibis might be foraging in the vegetation, or watch for families of ducks following their parents. Next up will be four large nests that are perched atop consecutive power-line poles. Ospreys peer down from their lofty positions as you cruise beneath the wires. When you've had enough of watching these regal birds, bear left out of the swamp and back to your car.

Prudence Island. *Distance:* 8 miles (loop). *Time:* 2 hours. *Difficulty:* Easy. *Directions:* The island is a 20-minute ferry ride from Church Street Wharf in Bristol. Call 401-253-9808 for times.

Until a few years ago, Prudence Island was one of the state's top destinations for walking. Miles of trails snaked through the undeveloped landscape, interrupted only by the occasional deer grazing by an old vineyard or apple orchard. However, with the deer came the dreaded Lyme Disease. Several people were infected, the media brought it to the public's attention, albeit in an exaggerated way, and Dear Prudence, no one came out to play. Hikers have avoided the trails and the meddlesome ticks ever since.

Mountain biking provides a different scenario. We can cruise on the dirt and gravel roads without having to venture too deep into the woods, and we're obviously going at a much faster pace. No nasty bug is going to attach itself to your body when you're cruising at 10 to 15 miles per hour. Take advantage of the empty roads. With no restaurants, hotels, or official camping sites on the island, very few tourists outside of sailors venture here. Traveling to Prudence Island is like visiting the Rhode Island of the 1850s, a combination of farmland, small villages, and spectacular ocean views around every bend.

This jaunt circles the southern end of the island, within South Prudence State Park. From the ferry landing in Homestead, veer left onto Narragansett Avenue and past the small lighthouse at Sandy Point. The road soon turns uphill, away from the village and the sea. When Narragansett veers right, go straight ahead on the secondary road and turn left at the T. This narrow path cruises down to the water along an old fence, put up during World War II for defense purposes. Narragansett Bay was thought to be one of the first places our adversaries would target if America was attacked. Follow the gravel lane as it laces the shores of the island. Through the brush, you can see Newport Bridge to the right and Mount Hope Bridge to the left. You'll soon pass the first of many underground ammunition bunkers.

At the next junction, veer left and follow the road to a long fishing pier. Continue to the right along the narrow trail until it intersects with a concrete road near another bunker. When the road veers right, bear to your left on a gravel path that hugs the shoreline. Wide-open vistas of the ocean soon appear. Turn right at a large garage and continue on the paved road, which soon becomes a gravel lane. When you reach the T intersection you visited earlier, veer left to get back to Narragansett Avenue and Homestead.

Road Biking

Rhode Island is one of the most densely populated states in the nation, second only to New Jersey. Thus the roads can be extremely congested. The following rides are fun in the summer, but far less crowded in the spring or fall.

Block Island. *Distance:* 13 miles (loop). *Time:* A full day. *Difficulty:* Easy. *Directions:* Catch the ferry from Galilee, Rhode Island, for the shortest ferry ride to Block Island. Call 401-783-4613 for times and costs. Ferries also leave from Newport and from New London, Connecticut.

Weathered houses bravely face the ocean's wrath atop small hillsides that are more reminiscent of Scotland than Rhode Island. Bluffs plummet to the water's edge and moors line the long stretch of beach. Inland, century-old stone walls and small blue-green ponds speckle the rolling terrain. This is Block Island, a small chunk of land that in shape resembles a lamb chop, 12 miles south of the mainland town of Galilee. The ferry ride takes a little more than an hour, leaving you the rest of the day to roam on two wheels, stop, and see all of the island's wondrous sights.

This ride is more a tour of the island than a strenuous workout. After disembarking in Old Harbor, turn left past the Victorian motels and continue straight around a statue. You will bear left in a clockwise manner for most of the trip. Almost immediately after leaving the town, small fields cropped with cedar shingle houses appear on the right, the vast ocean to the left. Cruising uphill, the red brick **Southeast Lighthouse** stands tall over the sea. You can stop to walk around the lighthouse, but I would continue a little farther to the **Mohegan Bluffs** parking lot. A small trail lined with raspberry and rose bushes leads to a majestic overlook where Mohegan's 200-foot cliffs fall to the sea. Another trail leads down to a beach where you are likely to feel inconsequential as you walk beneath massive sheets of rock.

Back on the bikes, turn left through a series of small ponds that are home to lily pads, frogs, and turtles. Ride past Center Road to Cooneymus Road where, at the intersection, you can usually find one of the numerous lemonade stands that appear on the island during the hot summer months. Bring lots of change to support the local adolescents. On Cooneymus, look for a sign for **Rodman's Hollow.** Here you can give your bikes a rest and walk on one of the Greenway trails through this forested glacial ravine to Black Rock Beach (see "Walks and Rambles"). When you return to the bikes, continue around the southwestern part of the island, turning left at the sign for **Chaplin's Marina.** Situated on Great Salt Pond's New Harbor, this is a good place to have lunch and watch the sailboats glide in and out of their slips.

When you reach Corn Neck Road, turn left to ride along the moors that line the most popular beach on Block Island, **Crescent Beach.** Just north of the beach, **Clay Head Nature Trail** meanders along red clay cliffs to a network of intricate hiking trails called The Maze. The road ends at Settler's Rock, where you can walk over the sand to the granite **North Lighthouse,** built in 1867. Return on Corn Neck Road to Old Harbor for the 7 o'clock ferry back to the real world.

East Bay Bicycle Path, at Providence. *Distance:* 29 miles (round-trip). *Time:* 3 to 4 hours. *Difficulty:* Easy. *Directions:* Take I-195 to Gano Street (exit 3) and turn left, proceeding past the Days Inn to India Point Park. Trail parking is available here.

All it takes is a mere 6 miles on a paved path to leave a highly industrialized section of Providence and reach the sheltered coastline of Narragansett Bay. No wonder locals would rather bike to the beach than deal with car traffic. The East Bay Bicycle Path (14.5 miles long, one way), built on the railbed of the former Providence/Worcester line, heads southeast from Providence along the scenic shores of the bay to the town of Bristol. Less than 2 miles into the ride, fishing trawlers and sailboats start to appear on the right and small inlets and wetlands can be seen on the left. In the warmer months, you're likely to see locals digging for littleneck clams in the shallow waters along the route. That's quite a contrast from the view of the Providence skyline that lurks behind you.

Soon the trail becomes far more suburban as cliffs line the bay-side, home to pelicans, egrets, and the occasional swan. South of River-side, the trail feels more secluded as you head through forest. Prior to mile 6 you will reach **Haines Park,** your first choice of beaches along the route. The trail then swerves inland through the town of Barring-ton and crosses two wooden bridges before reaching **Warren.** Just past the 10-mile mark, Warren is the best place to stock up on food and drink. South of Warren, the trail hugs the shoreline of Narragansett once again as the bay widens before reaching the ocean waters. Soon you'll be at **Colt State Park** and **Bristol Town Beach,** the finest spot for sunbathing along the route. The trail ends in Bristol at **Inde-pendence Park,** near a handful of seafood restaurants that undoubt-edly sell freshly caught littleneck clams.

Newport. *Distance:* 10 miles (loop). *Time:* 2 to 3 hours. *Difficulty:* Easy. *Directions:* From points east, follow Route 138 to Route 138A to Memorial Boulevard. Turn left on Bellevue Street. Parking is across the street from the International Tennis Hall of Fame. From Newport Har-bor, look for the signs to Bellevue Mansions.

Nowhere else on the Atlantic seaboard is opulence taken to the extravagant heights of the Newport mansions. This ride takes you on a road to riches (albeit not yours) before hugging the shoreline to Newport Harbor. Park your car and bear right down Bellevue Avenue. **Kingscote,** an 1839 Victorian mansion with Tiffany glass windows, is the first "cottage" to appear on this broad tree-lined street. The establishment was owned by George Noble Jones, one of the Southerners who summered in Newport. A left turn onto Ruggles will bring you to Newport's most elaborate summer home, **The Breakers,** constructed between 1892 and 1895 for Cornelius Vanderbilt, who died three years after his dream house was finished. Back on Bellevue, you'll pass **Château-sur-Mer** (built for William Wetmore, who amassed a fortune in the China trade), William Vanderbilt's sumptuous **Marble House,** and **Rosecliff,** the famed mansion designed by architect Stanford White in 1900 and seen in the film *The Great Gatsby*. At the Astors' **Beechwood,** actors portray servants and high-society guests in a lively reenactment of Newport's Gilded Age.

Follow Bellevue to the end, where there's a small turnaround at **Bailey's Beach.** Here you can see these mansions' magnificent backyards, the size of football fields, on the 3-mile-long Cliff Walk (see "Walks and Rambles"). Back on two wheels, veer left onto Ocean Avenue past the perfect crescent of sand known as Gooseberry Beach. Farther along is King's Beach and the rocky shoreline of Brenton Point State Park. Cattle grazing on manicured lawns signal your arrival at **Hammersmith Farm.** Jacqueline and John F. Kennedy held their wedding reception on these grounds and returned for numerous summer vacations. Go straight on Brenton Road to Halidon Street, which will you give you an unobstructed view of the yachts anchored in Newport Harbor. A right turn on Thames and left turns onto Narragansett and Bellevue will bring you back to the parking lot.

Tiverton–Little Compton. *Distance:* 29 miles (loop). *Time:* 3 to 4

Biking through Little Compton

hours. *Difficulty:* Easy to moderate. *Directions:* Park at the Stone Ridge Inn, located on Route 77 in Tiverton, south of Route 24.

While the crowds flock to Newport, the small stretch of land across the Sakonnet River is popular with Providencers and Bostonians who would prefer to keep Rhode Island's southeastern corner a coveted secret. Quintessential New England villages, more at home in Vermont, lie several miles inland from the harbors of Rhode Island Sound and the coastal marshes of the river.

After parking your car at the Stone Ridge Inn, turn left onto Route 77 for your first views of sailboats gliding along the harbor. A right turn across a small bridge onto Nannaquaket Road brings you past spacious dwellings with manicured yards sloping down to the river or woods. The road merges back to Route 77, where you turn right for a short run before veering right again onto Seapowet Road. On the right-hand side of Seapowet is the **Emilie Ruecker Wildlife Refuge.** Fiddler crabs and a vast assortment of seabirds are found on a quick walk along the salt marshes, rocky outcroppings, and uplands. Seapowet Road turns into Neck Road, which is lined on both sides by potato farms and small tidal pools. Before making a left turn onto Pond Bridge Road, you'll spot llamas grazing at a farm.

Pond Bridge Road ventures downhill to Route 77, where you turn right and continue south. On the stands that line Route 77, you can often find fresh fruit, baked bread, even homemade salsa and chips. Weighted down with goodies, pedal to **Sakonnet Point** at the end of Route 77 and picnic on the rocks overlooking this working harbor. Anglers fish off the large boulders, and sailboats tack around a lighthouse that overlooks Rhode Island Sound.

After a quick energy boost, venture back on Route 77 North, turning right on Swamp Road. Your first left brings you to a white steeple that towers over a perfectly designed village green. This is the town of

Little Compton. Continue past farmland to the road's end, where you turn left, climbing uphill to Route 77. Veering right, cruise on the shoulder of Route 77 all the way back to the Stone Ridge Inn.

Walks and Rambles

The following are three gems for walkers. You will also find other good walking opportunities at the wildlife refuges in the state (see "Birding"), some with trails along the shoreline that are ideal for an early morning stroll.

Napatree Point, near Watch Hill. *Distance:* 3 miles (round-trip). *Time:* 90 minutes. *Difficulty:* Easy. *Directions:* From Westerly, take Route 1A South and stay to the right as you make your way down to Watch Hill. When you see the sailboats on the right and the stores in town, find a parking spot.

For sand lovers, it doesn't get better than this wild coast walk that juts out of the southwestern corner of the state, rewarding you with views of Connecticut and Fishers Island, New York. Walk along the ocean wall before heading through a small gate. You can take off your shoes and socks now, because the soft sand trail leads directly to the beach. Listen to the sound of the waves as you glide along the water on this crescent-shaped beach all the way to the point.

The spit of land curves back toward Rhode Island, in a manner similar to Provincetown at the tip of Cape Cod. Sailboats cruise in Long Island Sound, ospreys and their young fly above the shores. As you reach the point, the last square foot of terra firma, the winds begin to howl, the surf seems a bit more ominous, and the sand changes to large battered rocks. You can see the breakwater that stretches from Westerly, the small harbor of Stonington, Connecticut, and the dome of Fishers Island. A foghorn moans in the distance. On the return trip, view the Victorian houses that cling to the bluffs of Watch Hill. Like Newport, Watch Hill is known for its old wealth, but the houses are far more reserved than the extravagant mansions on Bellevue Street.

The Greenway Trail, on Block Island. *Distance:* 5 miles (round-trip). *Time:* 3 hours. *Difficulty:* Easy. *Directions:* From Old Harbor, take Old Town Road and turn left onto Center Road. The small parking lot is located on the right-hand side of the road across from the airport at Nathan Mott Park. Maps are available from the Block Island Nature Conservancy, at 401-466-2129.

Remarkable as it might seem, tiny Block Island has some of the finest walks in the state. Called the Greenway, rarely another human is found (even in the hectic summer months) on these Nature Conservancy–maintained trails that wind from mid-island to the southeast coast. Park your bike and ramble away from the ruckus on a green spongy carpet that leads straight through a four-way junction to the **Enchant-ed Forest.** Appropriately named, this deep dark forest of red pines, spruces, and maples takes you back to the Block Island of yore.

Bear right to circle around Turnip Farm, a wide-open field of bushy rockrose, northern blazing star, and other, more prosaic wildflowers. Bear right again to cross the unpaved Old Mill Road. Bright yellow goldfinches, graceful marsh hawks, and brown and yellow butterflies, distinctive to Block Island, may be seen along this stretch of the trail. Before crossing Cooneymus Road and continuing to Rodman's Hollow, you'll spot a small house that mysteriously looks like a bookend.

Rodman's Hollow is a glacial cleft that is actually a sandy depres-sion in the land. Take the short loop walk atop a knoll for panoramic vistas of the surrounding hills, ocean, and old stone walls. From this vantage point, you could easily be in the British countryside. When you reach the **Black Rock Trail,** turn left to reach Black Rock Beach, on a remote cove dwarfed by high bluffs. Then simply turn around and start walking back.

Cliff Walk, at Newport. *Distance:* 6.5 miles (round-trip). *Time:* 2 to 3 hours. *Difficulty:* Easy. *Directions:* Take Route 138 South to Route 138A South to Newport. Turn right on Memorial Boulevard and park at Easton's Beach. The walk starts behind nearby Cliff Walk Manor. Tours are offered by the Cliff Walk Society, at 401-841-8770.

Rhode Island's most popular stroll is the Cliff Walk, a 3.2-mile walkway that follows the rugged Newport shoreline on one side, the backyards of the massive Bellevue Avenue mansions on the other. Start on the sidewalk behind Cliff Walk Manor and continue uphill above the ocean. Fences and hedges soon appear on the right, guarding the privacy of these 60- to 70-room summer "cottages." However, many of the backyards remain open to the sea and to us voyeurs. Most impressive is the sight of **The Breakers,** the Italian-style villa commissioned by Cornelius Vanderbilt. The manicured lawns of the mansion slope down to an open iron gate on the Cliff Walk. Another highlight is the Chinese-style teahouse at the **Marble House,** occupied by William and Alva Vanderbilt. You'll see the red and gold lacquered pagoda just before you walk through the first tunnel. When Alva Vanderbilt realized there was no means to boil tea inside the pagoda, she ordered that a small railroad be built from the main house so that her servants could quickly transport the tea before it got cold. Only God knows what happened to the poor servant who brought Alva a tepid pot of tea.

A second tunnel leads you to an area called Rough Point, where the ocean surf batters the boulders below. I usually turn around here, but you can continue along the rocky trail (which has replaced the sidewalk) to Ledge Road and return via shady Bellevue Avenue. This way, you can see both sides of the mansions.

TWO, IF BY SEA

Canoeing

The numerous ponds that dot Rhode Island are havens for canoeists and anglers. This is especially true of the coastal ponds, Ninigret in Charlestown and nearby Worden Pond in South Kingston. Flatwater kayaking is just as popular as canoeing, and a kayak might be easier to maneuver in tidal waters like these. If you don't own your own kayak, you can paddle the Narrow River with **Narrow River Kayaks** (95 Middlebridge Road, Narragansett; 401-789-0334). The river is an inlet on the western side of Narragansett Bay. Canoeists and kayakers can paddle upstream to Lower and Upper Pond or downstream around a small island to Pettaquamscutt Cove.

Ninigret Pond, at Charlestown. *Distance:* 2–4 miles. *Time:* 2 to 3 hours. *Difficulty:* Easy. *Directions:* To reach the Charlestown Breach-way, take the Charlestown Beach turnoff from Route 1 onto Narrow Lane. At the T, turn left onto Route 1A, following signs for the beach. After 0.2 mile, turn right. After another 1.3 miles, you'll see the eastern end of Ninigret Pond and the entrance to Charlestown Town Beach. Continue for another mile to the Breachway and a boat launch.

At 1,700 acres, Ninigret is the largest of Rhode Island's coastal ponds. While large size is usually an attraction for motorboats and a deterrent for paddlers, Ninigret offers a slew of activities in and out of the boat. You can paddle to the north shore from the Breachway (go with the incoming tide across the pond because the current is obviously strong) to reach the **Ninigret National Wildlife Refuge.** If you dock your canoe to the east of the refuge, as not to disturb nesting shorebirds, you can walk on the trails to view some of the 250 recorded bird species. Warblers enjoy the low-lying shrub vegetation,

Canoeing Ninigret Pond

like bayberry and beach plum. The salt marsh on the southwestern shores lead to Ninigret Conservation Area and the remote **East Beach.** Accessible only by foot and four-wheel drive, East Beach is a wild 3.5-mile-long stretch of dunes and sand on the Atlantic—the perfect place to lounge before heading back to the put-in.

Fishing

Whether you crave freshwater or saltwater fish, there's no lack of choice in Rhode Island. Surf-cast anywhere along the coast for stripers and blues. Some of the more popular places (from east to west) are the rocks of Sakonnet Point, Brenton Point in Newport, Beavertail State Park in Jamestown, the inlet to Ninigret Pond, Weekapaug Breachway in South County, and Point Judith near Galilee.

Point Judith is the best place to find party boats and charters, with more than 40 charter boats for six people or less serving the area. **Cap-**

tain Frank Blount (401-783-4988) has three boats taking anglers out on half-day, full-day, and night trips for cod, blues, porgies, blackfish, and flukes; he also has overnight trips where you can reel in pollock, tuna, bonita, and shark. Prices start at $20.

Captain Bud Phillips (401-635-4292) of Sakonnet Point Marina will bring parties of up to six on his 38-foot *Oceans.* In Newport, contact **Captain Jim Korney** (401-849-9642), skipper of *Fishin' Off,* for full- or half-day charters. The **Rhode Island Party and Charterboat Association** (401-737-5812) has information on prices and reservations statewide.

On Block Island, two of the best places to throw out your line are Sandy Point in the north end of the island and Black Rock in the southwest corner. John Swienton, an employee for more than 30 years at **Twin Maples bait and tackle shop** (401-466-5547), says the prize run for stripers usually starts around June 6 or 7, three to four weeks later than on the mainland because of colder water temperatures. Thus the season lasts longer, running well into the beginning of December. For bait he uses dark-colored needlefish for the beginning and end of the season, light-colored needlefish for the middle. **Captain Denny Dillon** (401-783-5644) charters boats for offshore fishing trips.

Freshwater gamefish include largemouth bass, chain pickerel, yellow perch, northern pike, and crappies. Brook, brown, and rainbow trout and landlocked salmon are also stocked in many of the rivers and ponds. Pawcatuck and Wood Rivers, along with a number of ponds such as Breakneck in Arcadia Management Area and Worden Pond near Kenyon, are known for their fishing. For more information, contact the Rhode Island Department of Environmental Management, **Division of Fish and Wildlife,** at 401-222-3075.

Sailing

Narragansett Bay's deep natural harbor is regarded as one of the finest cruising grounds in the Northeast. On any sunny afternoon, you're bound to see hundreds of full sails coasting up and down the bay. Marked by Newport at its southern tip, the bay is an estuary where saltwater arms are fed by freshwater streams and rivers. Come summer, the prevailing wind is the "smoky sou'wester," the same breeze that drew the America's Cup races to Rhode Island for more than 50 years, until America's defeat by Australia in 1983. Almost without exception, calm sunny mornings are followed by windy afternoons with the onshore breeze arriving between noon and 1 PM. By midafternoon, the wind can build to 25 knots or more, but the average speed is between 10 and 20 knots. Fair breezes and clear skies is the usual forecast in the summer and fog is less prevalent than in coastal Maine.

To escape Newport's crowds, cross the East Passage to find two largely undiscovered anchorages—**Jamestown Harbor** on the island of the same name and **Potter's Cove** at the north end of Prudence Island. Jamestown's historic waterfront is a great place to find a meal. Much of Prudence Island has remained wilderness, with a state park at the south end, the Prudence Conservatory in the center, and the Narragansett Bay National Estuarine Research Reserve at the north end. The island boasts more deer per square mile than any other spot in New England. The sail over to Block Island is popular with larger boats.

These days, there seem to be more sailing schools than sailors. But if you want to learn from the best, choose **J World** (1-800-343-2255; www.jworldschool.com). In a recent survey in *Practical Sailor*, J World won the highest ratings for its skilled instructors, challenging courses, and fleet of high-quality sailboats. Founded in 1982 in New-

J World Sailing School in Newport Harbor

port, J World has since added teaching facilities in San Diego, Annapolis, the Florida Keys, and Sweden. In Newport, J World adheres to the philosophy of "more time on the water, less time in the classroom" and will turn just about any landlubber into a sailing aficionado. The intensive course features six hours on the waters of Narragansett Bay every day on a J-24. You'll learn how to set the sails, tie knots, stop and start under sail, tack, jibe, and anchor.

Sail Newport (60 Fort Adams Drive, Newport; 401-846-1983) is based in Fort Adams State Park. They have 14 rental boats, J-22s and Rhodes 19s, that range in price from $35 to $153, depending on the day and amount of rental time; the boats are rented for three, six, or nine hours. Sail Newport also offers a three-day course of instruction, with prices ranging from $109 to $129, depending on whether you take the course on weekdays or weekends.

On Block Island, **The Block Island Club** (401-466-5939) offers sailing instruction to individuals or families. Lasers, sunfish, and JY-1s are available to members.

Scuba Diving

Newport Diving Center (550 Thames Street, Newport; 401-847-9293), arranges two-tank charters to many of the wrecks found on the floor of the bay. The dives usually range from 70 to 120 feet.

Sea Kayaking

While you still might see some wave action, the kayakers on the western half of Narragansett Bay face far less boat traffic. The **Kayak Centre** (401-295-4400; www.kayakcentre.com) in the historic town of Wickford will take you on a three-hour tour past the yachts in the outlying harbor, through the oyster beds and sea grass meadows that make up the puckered shoreline. Along the way, you'll see century-old houses, a few fishermen, and Rabbit and Cornelius Islands in the middle of the bay. The Kayak Centre also offers full-moon paddles, a sunset paddle at Ninigret Pond (see "Canoeing"), and a 12-mile jaunt to Block Island.

For those leery of the chop in Wickford Harbor, try paddling the brackish and marsh-fringed Narrow River. Rent boats at **Narrow River Kayaks** (95 Middlebridge Road, Narragansett; 401-789-0334) to venture along the river to Narragansett Town Beach and the wide open sea. Strong paddlers can make it to Beaver Tail State Park at the southern tip of Jamestown Island in less than an hour.

In Tiverton, **Sakonnet Boathouse** (169 Riverside Drive; 401-624-1440; www.sakonnetboathouse.com) provides rentals, guided tours, and clinics. You can choose from dozens of half-day and full-day trips, including such activities as exploring the islands of Bluebell Cove, watching ospreys dive for fish along the Westport River, meeting the quahogging fleet in Mount Hope Bay, taking in the waterfront homes of Bristol, or paddling along the Sakonnet River to explore the Emily Rueker Wildlife Refuge and Seapowet Marsh Wildlife Preserve.

Oceans & Ponds (401-466-5131) is the only place to rent kayaks on Block Island. Some of the finest fishing spots on Block, like Black Rock, are impossible to reach via car or bike. Simply rent a kayak and you'll view coastline that few locals have ever seen.

Surfing

Narragansett Town Beach and Second Beach in Middletown are two of the best spots to catch waves. Locals also four-wheel it to East Beach, near Charlestown, to catch the early morning action. Waves rarely exceed 2 feet, except when one of those tropical depressions climbs up the eastern seaboard. **The Watershed** (409 Main Street, Wakefield; 401-789-3399; surf phone, 401-789-1954) rents boards for Narragansett and gives lessons every Wednesday at noon.

Wind Surfing

Ninigret Pond near Charlestown and Narragansett Town Beach are the two best places on the Rhode Island coast to wind surf. **Sail Newport** (60 Fort Adams Drive, Newport; 401-846-1983) offers eight one-week classes to youths during the summer; cost is $170 per week. Sailboards and instruction are also available from **Island Sports** (86 Aquidneck Avenue, Middletown; 401-846-4421).

A DAY AT THE BEACH

The white sand beaches and grassy dunes of Rhode Island entice visitors who want to bask in the sun and swim in the warm surf. Yes, I said warm surf. While the waters of Maine, New Hampshire, and Cape

Cod remain frigid in August, the waters of Rhode Island can be a balmy 65 to 70 degrees Fahrenheit. Yet the choice of beach on Little Rhody's 420-mile coastline can be daunting. The state's official map lists 69 ocean beaches. Starting from the southwest in South County and heading east, the beaches begin with **Watch Hill Town Beach,** popular with summer visitors who come to this Victorian town. The gentle surf is good for young children. Far more wild is the barrier beach that lines Napatree Point (see "Walks and Rambles"), with the beach walk starting behind Watch Tree's century-old carousel. This narrow spit of land has far more migratory shorebirds than beachcombers.

Several miles east of Watch Hill, **Misquamicut State Beach** is arguably Rhode Island's best honky-tonk beach. Seven miles of ocean frontage are backed by Atlantic Avenue's hotels, bars, restaurants, amusement centers, water slides, miniature golf courses, you name it. The surf has minimal undertow, so it's good for families. And there's ample parking with a 3,000-car lot and many more spaces available on Atlantic Avenue.

Near the end of East Beach Road and Route 1 in Charlestown is **Blue Shutters Town Beach.** The small beach is ideal for families, with showers, snack bar, and acres of expansive coastline with views across the sound to Block Island. Two miles away is another Rhode Island gem, **East Beach,** where the ever-present wind is perfect on a hot summer's day. Sunbathers and boogie boarders favor the wild Atlantic side, while canoers and wind surfers opt for the blue waters of Ninigret Pond (see "Canoeing"). On the pond's northwestern shore, 400-acre Ninigret National Wildlife Refuge has a network of trails that attracts birders.

East Matunuck State Beach in South Kingstown, at the end of Succotash Road, is a favorite among singles. The beach has a long gradual drop that makes for good bodysurfing. Afterward, everyone heads to the classic Ocean Mist beach bar in Matunuck to have a couple cool beers and listen to live music—everything from Cajun swing to country rock.

Roger Wheeler Memorial State Park Beach in Galilee is shielded from the open sea by a rock jetty. The gentle surf, the tamest on Narragansett Bay, is the perfect place for young children who dare not dodge the waves. There's also a playground and a refreshment stand. On the other hand, just south of Narragansett, **Scarborough State Beach** has a pounding surf. Bodysurfers ride the waves while landlubbers hit the boardwalk, lined with concessions selling fried clams, burgers, and much more.

The half-mile-long **Narragansett Town Beach** is within walking distance from the hotels and restaurants on Route 1A. Families share the wide expanse of fine sand with surfers who relish the slow-breaking waves. Indeed, surfers don wet suits in the fall and take over the beach when the sun worshipers are long gone.

In Newport, families venture to **Easton's Beach,** with its gradual drop-off and small aquarium. It's the town's largest public beach, with more than 700 parking spots. Bailey's Beach, at the east end of the Cliff Walk, is where the tony go to tan. Come by foot or bike, since there's no parking here. Nearby, **Second Beach** in Middletown has a hopping singles scene. The long stretch of dunes and sand runs between Hanging Rock and Sachuest Point. **Third Beach** is a protected shore on the baylike Sakonnet River that's good for youngsters.

Grinnell's Beach in Sakonnet is a quarter-mile stretch of sand where local teens tend to hang out. **Gaspee Point Beach** in Warwick is a secluded spot good for children. Finally, on Block Island, **Fred Benson Town Beach** is part of the much larger Crescent Beach.

CAMPGROUNDS

Oak Embers Campground, West Greenwich (401-397-4042). From the junction of Routes 3 and 165 in Austin, drive a little over 5 miles west on Route 165 and turn right on Escoheag Hill Road. Continue for 1.5 miles to the campground. The facility offers 60 sites (37 with water and electricity), hot showers, flush toilets, a swimming pool, and a store. The campground is adjacent to 13,817-acre Arcadia Management Area, and campers can choose between two swimming lakes, freshwater fishing, and many miles of mountain biking and hiking trails.

Worden Pond Family Campground, near Wakefield (401-789-9113). From the junction of Routes 1 and 110 in Perryville, head 2 miles north on Route 110 and turn left onto Worden Pond Road. Continue for a mile to the campground. Here are 200 sites (some with water and electrical hook-ups), hot showers, flush toilets, and a store. With the campground situated on the southern shore of the state's largest freshwater lake, you can spend your day swimming, canoeing, or fishing. You're also just a 10-minute drive to the beaches.

Burlingame State Park, near Charlestown (401-322-7994). Located on Route 1, 4 miles west of Charlestown. The park provides 755 sites (no hook-ups), hot showers, a grocery store, and firewood. Most of the sites are situated on the shores of Watchaug Pond, and the Atlantic is only a few miles away. The gigantic complex, also open to trailers, is always crowded due to its proximity to the ocean.

Charlestown Breachway (401-364-7000). From Charlestown, head south on Charlestown Beach Road. There are 75 sites for self-contained trailer units (no hook-ups) and flush toilets. Simply a sand parking lot, the location of this site couldn't get much better. Swim on either the ocean or Ninigret Pond side, both a short walk away. You can also surf-cast for stripers, canoe or wind surf the pond, or walk the trails of Ninigret National Wildlife Refuge.

Fishermen's Memorial State Park, near Narragansett (401-789-8374). From Narragansett, head south on Point Judith Road, near Galilee. You'll find 182 sites (40 full hook-ups; 107 with water and electricity), flush toilets, hot showers, and a children's playground. From the well-groomed grounds, it's a short walk to Wheeler Memorial Beach or Salty Brine State Beach. You're also close to the Block Island ferry at Galilee.

Fort Getty Recreation Area, Jamestown (401-423-7264). Take either the Jamestown or Newport Bridges to Route 138 South and head south on North Main Road. Turn right onto Narragansett Avenue, then left onto Southwest Avenue as it merges into Beavertail Road. Turn right onto Fort Getty Road to the campground. There are 125 sites (100 with water and electricity), flush toilets, hot showers, a boat ramp, and a fishing dock. There's plenty of saltwater recreation to be had at Fort Getty State Park, situated near the historic town of Jamestown on Conanicut Island in Narragansett Bay.

Melville Pond Campground, Portsmouth (401-849-8212). From the junction of Routes 138 and 114 in Portsmouth, drive 1.7 miles south on Route 114 and turn right on Stringham Road. Go half a mile, then turn right on Sullivan Road and go another half mile to the campground. The facility provides 123 sites (33 with full hook-ups; 33 with water and electricity), handicapped-accessible rest rooms, flush toilets, hot showers, firewood. The closest campground to Newport, these sites offer campers easy access to Narragansett Bay.

CHAPTER THREE

Massachusetts:
Cape Cod and the Islands

▶ Ever since the *Mayflower* sailed into a harbor at the eastern end of Cape Cod on November 11, 1620, settlers have been trying to subsist on the land's meager offerings. The pitch pine forests were exploited for their wood and resin content, trees were tapped for turpentine and sap, and the oak forests were cut down in favor of farmland. The colonists failed to foresee the dire consequences. Without vegetation, blustery ocean squalls forced sand drifts to form in the most inconvenient places—within harbors, atop cobblestone streets, and, ironically, on the farmland the people were trying to cultivate.

By the late 1700s, many of the natives had left their dying fields and looked out toward the sea. With prices of whale oil, spermaceti, and baleen surging upward, whaling had become a most lucrative profession. Nantucket's population swelled to 10,000 during the whaling days, becoming the third-largest city in Massachusetts, after Boston and Salem. The cod and mackerel fishery supported about two thousand families on the Cape, almost one-third of the population. Successful captains brought home treasures and large amounts of money, a result of the prosperous maritime economy. Other unfortunate souls left their ships on the shores, wrecked on the treacherous shoals that

The Cape Cod Bay beaches

line the Cape's coastline. When fishing and whaling went into a state of decline in 1860, people found it hard to make a living. As a result of deforestation, the Cape was one immense sand dune. So-called wreckers earned a living by scouring the beach for shipwrecks, to sell the remains as driftwood.

At the turn of the 20th century, the Cape experienced a remarkable turnaround. Forests were replanted, the railroad made farming economically viable by shipping produce to Boston and New York, and the Cape Cod Canal opened in 1914, reducing the number of shipping disasters because boats no longer needed to travel around the tip of Provincetown. The most significant impact, however, was tourism. Visitors started arriving in the 1920s and have never stopped. With the large number of summer homes, the populations on the Cape, Martha's Vineyard, and Nantucket now increase exponentially each July and August.

This does not mean that one can't walk for miles on desolate beaches or sail to uninhabited harbors. There are still remote spots on the Cape where the serenity of sand meeting sea is enhanced by the cacophony of birds singing—goldfinches, swallows, and Savannah sparrows are among the hundreds of species in flight. The mesmerizing force of nature may be interrupted only by an occasional greeting from a clam digger or fisherman who has left his cedar-shingled house to probe his vast front yard, his face wizened, his hands callused, and his eyes watery, pale blue, like the ocean he knows so well.

On the Vineyard and Nantucket, it's more of a challenge to find your own stretch of shoreline, but peruse these pages and ye shall find privacy, even in summer. Whatever season or sport you choose, the salty sea will never be far away, pervading your senses and leaving a feeling of tranquility in its wake.

THE TERRAIN

> Far below us was the beach, with a long line of breakers rushing
> to the strand. The sea was exceedingly dark and stormy, and the
> wind seemed to blow not so much as the exciting cause, as from
> sympathy with the already agitated ocean. The waves broke on
> the bars at some distance from the shore, ten or twelve feet high,
> like a thousand waterfalls, then rolled in foam to the sand. There
> was nothing but that savage ocean between us and Europe.
>
> —Henry David Thoreau, *Cape Cod*

Sand and sea; these are the images that appear when we think of Cape
Cod. Undulating dunes and long stretches of fine white beach serve as
soft welcome mats for the angry surf that rolls ashore. Looking at a
map, the Cape looks like the flexed arm of a body builder, the shoulder at Buzzards Bay, the elbow at Chatham, the wrist at Truro, and
the fist at Provincetown. The Cape's unique formation—along with
that of the two largest nearby islands, Nantucket and Martha's Vineyard—owes its existence to a melting glacier ice front. When the ice
retreated, rock debris of all kinds was released to form a terminal
moraine, a high pile of sand, clay, and boulders. Bordering the
moraines on the ocean side were gently sloping outwash plains and
small irregular depressions in the land called kettleholes.

Over thousands of years, the constant battering of the surf created long sandy beaches, soft cliffs, and bluffs. Today the beaches are
an extensive network of dunes, barrier beaches, long sand spits, and
barrier islands. Salt marshes and tidal estuaries are protected from
the impact of ocean currents by the sand. Inland, the kettleholes have
been filled with rainwater to create ponds and, surprisingly, woodlands
have grown from the poor sandy soil.

When Captain John Smith published *A Description of New England*

NOTED NATURALISTS OF CAPE COD

"Wishing to get a better view than I had yet had of the ocean.... I made a visit to Cape Cod in October, 1849." Thus, began the account of Henry Thoreau's adventures in the book *Cape Cod*. Better known for the two years he spent at Walden Pond and his essay *Civil Disobedience*, Thoreau walked the coastline from Eastham to Provincetown three times, in 1849, 1850, and 1855. He compared crossing the barren and desolate landscape to "traveling a desert." Indeed, the Cape in the mid-1800s was one massive sand dune due to deforestation. In his dissertations on the Cape, Thoreau was particularly fascinated with oystermen and wreckers, people who searched the beach for driftwood and fragments of wrecked vessels. The interaction of these people was, he writes, of a "nature that was hostile and indifferent to human life," one that forced Cape Codders to eke out a living from the barren shores and stormy seas.

Henry Beston followed Thoreau's path to Cape Cod. In *The Outermost House,* Beston describes his experience of living in a house on the dunes of Eastham between 1926 and 1927. Beston lived alone, two miles from his nearest neighbor, so he could "observe carefully, brood long, and write slowly." Hmmm, I guess deadlines weren't much of an issue back then. Beston explored the "relation of nature to the human spirit." Contrary to Thoreau, he was only interested in his own isolated spirit and the consequences the ocean would have on him. His book has more of a naturalistic tone, explicitly describing the way sea and beach change during the different seasons. By the 1920s, trees were reappearing on the Cape, people no longer needed to scour the beach for firewood, and tourists were starting to arrive by train and automobile. Thoreau's statement that "the time will come when this coast will be a resort" was an astute prophecy.

in 1616, he portrayed the interior of Cape Cod as "onely a headland of high hils of sand overgrowne with shrubby pines, hurts [huckleberries], and such trash." Not much has changed. Scrub forests of oaks and pitch pine cover the hillside. In areas where the soil receives better moisture, thickets of red maples and hickories are found. Yet the beeches, birches, and maples that form dense forests throughout most of New England are few and far between here.

Plant and shrub life is also scarce, with heaths being the most notable exception. Blueberries, huckleberries, and sheep laurel grow in the dry woodlands, while cranberries and azaleas thrive in the wet boggy sections of the countryside. The cranberries have adapted so well to Cape Cod's acrid soil that they have become one of the region's few lucrative crops and a multimillion-dollar industry. On the island of Nantucket, Scotch heather and heath were introduced to the moorland in the mid-19th century and now grow naturally all over the island. American holly, popular in Christmas decorations, can be found at two preserves on Cape Cod.

GETTING HERE

Access to the 70-mile-long arm of **Cape Cod** is accomplished via two bridges that span Cape Cod Canal. The Bourne Bridge connects with Route 28 South to Falmouth. The more popular Sagamore Bridge connects with Route 6, the Cape's main thoroughfare. During Friday and Sunday evenings in the summer, Route 6 and the rotaries leading to the bridges are heavily congested. I would avoid these times at all cost. If Provincetown is your destination, consider taking the ferry direct from Boston. Bay State Cruises (617-748-1428; www.provincetownfast ferry.com) runs the *MV Provincetown II* daily from late June through Labor Day.

The best place to catch a ferry to the island of **Martha's Vineyard** is Woods Hole, off Route 28 on the Cape, or New Bedford, where you don't have to cross one of the bridges to get to Cape Cod. If you're planning to spend more than a day on the Vineyard, a car is advisable to get to the more remote areas of the island like Chappaquiddick and Gay Head.

From Hyannis, off Route 6, you can fly or take a ferry to **Nantucket.** The island of Nantucket is small enough that a car is not necessary.

The Activities

ONE, IF BY LAND

Birding

Not only is the interior of Cape Cod populated with cardinals, towhees, mockingbirds, catbirds, goldfinches, and woodpeckers, but its birds of the shore also entice many a visitor here. Shorebirds by the hundreds of thousands, returning from their Arctic breeding grounds, stop along Cape shores for many weeks as they fatten up for the rest of their long journeys south. Many of the hot spots to view these visitors are around Chatham—the tip of Morris Island, Monomoy National Wildlife Refuge, and South Beach. Other places where birds congregate are at the Massachusetts Audubon Society's Wellfleet Bay Sanctuary (see "Walks and Rambles") and at various sites within the Cape Cod National Seashore.

Shorebirds include oystercatchers, stilts, avocets, plovers, turnstones, sandpipers, and phalaropes. To see the birds well, it really helps to have binoculars, especially for those feathered friends that remain at a considerable distance. Bird field guides, binoculars, spotting scopes, and tripods can be found at **Bird Watcher's General Store** (36 Route 6A, Orleans; 508-255-6974).

You can join one of the many groups led by professional birders that visit the best viewing spots. The *Cape Cod Times* publicizes these trips, and the Audubon Society's **Wellfleet Bay Sanctuary** (508-349-2615), the **Cape Cod Museum of Natural History** in Brewster (508-896-3867), and the **Cape Cod National Seashore** (508-255-3421) have information about the trips.

To get to the tip of **Morris Island** in Chatham, start at the Chatham lighthouse and take Morris Island Road. After crossing the causeway, a sign will point you to the headquarters building of the Monomoy National Wildlife Refuge at the first left turn. From this building, walk down the long stairway to the beach, turn right, and walk to the very end of Morris Island. To see the greatest number of birds, go at low tide.

Martha's Vineyard is known for its piping plovers, trumpeter swans, red-tailed hawks, sandpipers, even bald eagles. Some of the best birding areas include Wasque Reservation and Cape Pogue in Chappaquiddick, Cedar Trees Neck Sanctuary, and Long Point Refuge.

Piping plovers can also be found at Great Point on **Nantucket** among numerous least and common terns, marsh hawks, and American oystercatchers. Sanford Farm is a good place to spot ospreys and red-tailed hawks.

The following section describes what is arguably the finest birdwatching spot in the whole region.

Monomoy National Wildlife Refuge, at Chatham. Both the Cape Cod Museum of Natural History and the Wellfleet chapter of the Massachusetts Audubon Society offer three-hour guided trips to North Monomoy Island in the summer to visit this refuge. The refuge consists of North and South Monomoy Islands and a portion of Morris Island.

Its 2,750 acres are predominantly barrier beaches of sand dunes, fresh-water ponds, and saltwater and freshwater marshes. The guided tour is highly recommended for anyone with an appreciation of nature, not just for the avid birdwatcher.

A seven-minute boat ride from Chatham drops you off on the shores of North Monomoy Island. Back in 1959, the island was still part of the Cape, but a tumultuous storm and the constant battering of waves severed this barrier beach from the mainland. Years later, more rough weather split the island in two. You'll disembark and slow-ly make your way around the island.

Herring gulls occupy much of the island's interior, but fortunately they make room for other species, like the American oystercatcher. This bird's orange beak makes it look like it has a carrot sticking out of its mouth. You'll also spot several species of sandpipers and black-bellied plovers. Then there are the swift willets, black cormorants fly-ing in V-formation, and the graceful northern harriers (marsh hawks), who seem to fly on auto-cruise. One of the most exciting viewings is not on land, but at sea. Harbor seals play with the sea kayakers who circumnavigate the island. The seals' playful heads bob up and down like lobster buoys.

Plan to wear a hat and a pair of shoes that can get wet (which they will). Price of the guided tour is $35.

Golf

There are more than 45 golf courses on the Cape, and about 20 of them are open to the public. Arguably the best public course is the **Ocean Edge Resort** course in Brewster (508-896-5911). The par-4 second hole is a 425-yard-long, uphill approach to a small green. Beware of the grass-lined pot bunkers protecting the green, which have steep sides and treacherous lies.

Close to the Ocean Edge Resort, and also designed by Brian Silva, is the **Captains Golf Course** (1000 Freeman's Way, Brewster; 508-896-1716). In 1999, Silva redesigned the original 18 holes and added 18 more.

Cape Cod's oldest golf course, the 9-hole **Highland Links Golf Club** in North Truro (Highland Road; 508-487-9201), dates back to 1892. Federally owned and town-run, the Highland Links course is gnarly and fun, played in slim corridors between sticker bushes and knee-high hay. Take note of signs that say "Danger! Sliding cliffs. Keep back." Five years ago, the lighthouse had to be moved because of eroding sand.

Then there's the **New Seabury Country Club** in Mashpee (508-539-8322), with its recent renovations: The Dunes Course has been lengthened by 300 yards, and the Ocean Course has flipped nines, moving the holes on the water to the back side.

On the Vineyard, **Farm Neck Golf Club** in Oak Bluffs (508-693-3057) is highly regarded. It's one of the most scenic courses in New England—but remember that President Clinton never broke 80 here.

Hiking

Great Island Trail. *Distance:* 7 miles (round-trip). *Time:* 3 to 4 hours. *Difficulty:* Strenuous. *Directions:* From Route 6, head into Wellfleet Center, taking a left on East Commercial Street and a right at the marina onto Chequessett Neck Road. There will be a sign for Great Island several miles down the road on the left. A map is available from Cape Cod National Seashore headquarters in South Wellfleet (508-349-3785).

Cape Cod National Seashore's longest trail, the Great Island Trail, is worthy of being designated a hike, not a walk. This hike through marsh, woods, and soft sand can be a strenuous thigh-burner. The trail follows the circumference of Great Island, a former whaling port and

Walking the Great Island Trail

now one of the most secluded areas in Cape Cod. For the serious walker who yearns to get away from the summer crowds, this path should not be missed. Bring several bottles of water, a hat, sunscreen, and perhaps a picnic lunch, and you're on your way.

Stroll down the short hill from the parking lot and take a right, continuing around the marsh. This small strip of sand is called The Gut, the other side being Great Island itself. At the fork, take a left toward **Smith Tavern.** Just before reaching the easternmost tip of the island, where people often fish for stripers and blues, you'll see a sign directing you over the dunes and through the woods. The trail winds through the pine forest to the site of an original whaling tavern. However, you'll have to use your imagination since there is only a small plaque here now. Just picture ole Pegleg banging his way to the bar of the Smith Tavern, smelling god-awful from bathing in whale oil and shouting to the bartender, "Give me another whiskey!" If this image doesn't work, look for red fox. When I was here last, I saw this golden sheen of fur whisk by me with something in its mouth—most likely a jackrabbit.

The Smith Tavern trail catches up with the main trail where you take a left. Continue out of the woods to a marsh where sand dunes tower on your right and Wellfleet Harbor can be seen to your left. This soft, sandy path leads up to Great Beach Hill. Five minutes later, you'll reach another marsh and a sand spit known as Jeremy Flats. At low tide, you can walk out to the tip, but I'd save your energy. You have a 2.2-mile walk down the beach of Cape Cod Bay to get back to The Gut.

I have rarely seen another person on this desolate strip of sand— usually just large scallop shells and tiny fiddle crabs: funny-looking critters who have one oversized claw bigger than their entire body. If you start to feel like Lawrence of Arabia lost in the desert, look out at 10 o'clock and you'll see Provincetown's Pilgrim Monument, a symbol of civilization. Thankfully you won't have to walk that far. Just take a right at the first staircase over the dunes and then take a left back to the parking lot. Don't forget to stretch.

Mountain Biking

Trail of Tears, near West Barnstable. *Distance:* Variable. *Time:* 1 to 2 hours. *Difficulty:* Strenuous. *Terrain:* Steep hills. *Directions:* Take Route 6 to exit 5. Take Route 149 South for several seconds before you take a quick right on the service road. Parking is available on the left under the huge power lines.

So you think Cape Cod is flat, without benefit of any good hills to rock your mountain bike. Hah! You have yet to try the aptly named Trail of Tears. Located on Barnstable Conservation Lands, this hellish trail was devised by motocross motorcyclists before they were booted off the grounds. Now the trail remains to test the skills of so-called expert mountain bikers. Go for it!

Start riding under the power lines and then take your second left. Within moments, you're huffing and puffing up a steep hill before cruising down singletracks with very little leeway to maneuver. You're looking at another hill as soon as you touch bottom, and before you know it, you're coasting down again. The cycle is unrelenting: up, down, up, down, until you make it out of this area 30 to 45 minutes later, sweating like a sprinkler system.

If your legs feel like Jell-O, take a right on the doubletrack path and head back to the parking lot. But if you still want more, take a left and cross the power lines twice before ending up where you started. If you get lost, simply take the power lines back to the parking lot or ask for directions from any of the other masochists.

Mashpee River Woodlands, near East Falmouth. *Distance:* 5 miles (loop). *Time:* 1 hour. *Difficulty:* Easy to moderate. *Terrain:* Rolling hills. *Directions:* From Falmouth, take Route 28 toward Hyannis. Then, 1.5 miles after the traffic rotary, take a sharp right onto Quinaquisset Avenue. Pass the sign on the right for the Mashpee River Wood-lands/North Parking Lot and continue until you reach Mashpee Neck Road. Turn right and look for a small parking lot and another Mashpee River Woodlands sign.

The singletrack trail through the Mashpee River Woodlands is a good hour-long ride for any mountain biker, regardless of level. The path loops along the Chickadee Trail before joining the main trail that borders the Mashpee River. Only the occasional fallen branch breaks up the flow of this rolling forest. Don't veer left on the main trail unless you want to stop at several overlooks. At the northern end, the trail loops around the Partridge Trail before meeting up with the main trail and the return trip to the parking lot. This route is a great workout to start or end your day.

Punkhorn Parklands, near Brewster. *Distance:* Varies. *Time:* 1 to 2 hours. *Difficulty:* Easy to moderate. *Directions:* From Brewster, follow Route 6A west toward Dennis. Take a left at Stony Brook Road (a blinking light) and another left onto Run Hill Road. The sign and makeshift parking lot are located on the left side of the road.

The maze of hiking trails that weave in and out of the 1,000-acre Punkhorn Parklands are challenging for bikers as well. Go early or late in the day, though, to avoid flattening hikers or being flattened by horseback riders. The Punkhorns were once sheep-grazing land and an active cranberry-producing area before the town of Brewster purchased the land and turned it over to the public.

From the so-called parking lot, follow the doubletrack main trail into the woods, making a right turn at the blue hiking sign. This trail rolls down into a bowl of mixed hardwoods and then curves back uphill to the main doubletrack. To the left of the main trail are singletracks that lead down to a small pond. Cruise down to the water and around the pond, ending up under the power lines, which lead back to your car. Take any trail you want and have fun, because it's almost impossible to get lost in this small thicket of trees.

Martha's Vineyard State Park. *Distance:* Varies. *Time:* Up to you. *Difficulty:* Easy. *Terrain:* Relatively flat. *Directions:* From Vineyard Haven, take Edgartown Road south and go right at the blinking light onto Airport Road. Park headquarters are on the left.

The most exciting part of mountain biking is creating your own trail. There's an incredible degree of freedom in any sport that lets you get lost in the woods and then find your way back. Thus there's a certain challenge in writing about mountain biking. I could describe in detail the route I took, but then you would stop every five minutes to follow my directions—and get lost in the same way that I did. That's no fun. Find your own trail and keep the spontaneity in the sport.

This is especially true of a place like Martha's Vineyard State Park (also called Manuel F. Correlus State Park). More than four thousand acres of pines, oaks, and low-lying scrub are crisscrossed by miles of fire roads, doubletrack bike trails, and singletrack trails. The fire roads follow a strict north-south and east-west pattern, so it's relatively easy to find your way back to the parking lot. Except for several small hills at the northeastern corner, the ride is relatively flat, but watch out for heavy sand drifts that will cause you to fishtail. From the parking lot, you can ride across Airport Road to play in the western part of the forest. You can ride for as long and as hard as you like. Just don't try to explain your route to anybody else.

The **Vineyard Off-Road Biking Association** meets every Sunday at 9 AM at West Tisbury's old Agricultural Hall for a three- to four-hour ride, open to the public. The bikers cruise on Land Bank and Ancient Way trails that only locals could know about. Call David Whitmon at 508-693-4905 to check it out.

Road Biking

The Cape Cod Rail Trail (described below) is one of the most popular bike paths in New England. However, it's the islands that I love to cruise upon. Biking is the best way to see Nantucket and Martha's Vineyard: You can explore the less-traveled side roads before resting on a stretch of sand only the natives know about.

East Island Route, Martha's Vineyard. *Distance:* 20 miles (loop). *Time:* 3 to 5 hours. *Difficulty:* Easy to moderate. *Directions:* Take the ferry from Woods Hole or New Bedford to Vineyard Haven on Martha's Vineyard.

The short hills, limited car traffic, and bike trails of Martha's Vineyard attract a growing number of bikers each year. If you only have a short amount of time, but want to test your legs, try the East Island Route. This ride is a great workout, yet far less challenging than the ride to Gay Head. The route takes you through the historic towns of Oak Bluffs and Edgartown before reaching the nature preserves of Chappaquiddick Island.

Once you disembark the ferry at Vineyard Haven, go left onto Beach Road and head toward Oak Bluffs. A mile into the journey, take a left at the sign for **East Chop** and follow the road past the million-dollar homes and the picture-perfect East Chop lighthouse before cruising down to **Oak Bluffs.** Pedal through town to the coastline and turn right. You'll soon approach a bike path that winds through Joseph Sylvia State Beach. Bike traffic here can be heavy in the summer months and the sea breeze can be fierce, so be aware.

Eventually, you'll reach **Edgartown,** which is a fine place to stop for lunch and wander around. The charming one-minute ferry ride to **Chappaquiddick Island** is at the edge of town. Continue on Chappaquiddick Road for 2.7 miles and you'll reach a dirt trail called Dyke Road. The road passes a Japanese-style garden called **Mytoi,** which is worth a stop. Azaleas, daffodils, dogwoods, and rhododendrons line the freshwater creeks in this three-acre garden.

The dirt road continues over the bridge that Ted Kennedy made infamous, before stopping at **East Beach.** Lock up your bikes and walk over the dunes to see one of the most pristine stretches of beach on the Atlantic coastline. Part of the Cape Pogue Wildlife Refuge, this barrier beach is perhaps the best place to bird-watch on the Vineyard. Ospreys, oystercatchers, piping plovers, terns, and the occasional bald eagle nest here.

Return to Edgartown via the same road and short ferry ride. You'll pass through town again before veering left on Vineyard Haven–Edgartown Road. This bike path is less scenic than the Oak Bluffs beach path, yet far more direct. There's a short hill on the way into Vineyard Haven, just in case you've felt this loop was an underachievement.

Bikes can be rented in Vineyard Haven, right off the ferry.

Gay Head Ride, Martha's Vineyard. *Distance:* 40 miles (loop). *Time:* 3 to 6 hours. *Difficulty:* Moderate to strenuous. *Directions:* Take the ferry from Woods Hole or New Bedford to Vineyard Haven on Martha's Vineyard.

The ride from Vineyard Haven to Gay Head Cliffs is not for the casual biker. It's for biking aficionados who want the challenge of a hilly ride close to 40 miles long. Pedal up South Main Street and continue on the equally crowded State Street. Take a left onto Old County Road for one of the most pleasant rides in the Vineyard. Farms line the right side of the road while the state forest sits on the left. Take a right onto Edgartown Road, past the tranquil town of West Tisbury, before making another right onto Music Street. Your first left will be Middle Road, a rolling road with little traffic through farmlands and green pastures. Eventually you'll end up in the small town of Chilmark.

Continue on South Road, stopping at the lookout over Menemsha Pond and the fishing village of the same name. Shift to low gears up the hill and then veer left at Moshup Trail, which will take you all the way to **Gay Head Cliffs.** You can walk up the hill to the lighthouse for a spectacular vista of the rainbow-colored clay or head down to the beach for a refreshing swim and hike (see "Walks and Rambles").

To return to Vineyard Haven, take a left onto Lighthouse Road and another left onto West Basin Road. Here, wait for Hughie Taylor and his boat to pick you up and bring you on a one-minute voyage to **Men-**

Seeking shells by the Gay Head cliffs

emsha. The price is $2. (Note: The boat runs only during the peak summer period. If you are biking at any other time, you will have to backtrack to Chilmark and go left on Menemsha Cross Road to get to this pristine village). If you're still hungry, stop in Menemsha at **Poole's fish market** or **Larsens' fish market** for incredibly fresh steamers, oysters on the half shell, or fish cakes.

The route continues on North Road, which connects with State Road and leads you back to the starting point. (For those of you whose legs are not yet weary, take a left at Lambert's Cove Road, off State Road, for a scenic route that loops around several ponds before returning to State Road.)

Nantucket. *Distance:* 23 miles (loop). *Time:* 3 hours. *Difficulty:* Easy to moderate. *Directions:* Fly or take the ferry to Nantucket town.

Nantucket's fairly flat terrain is ideal for road biking. Indeed, traveling on two wheels is the best way to get around and see the island's well-known cranberry bogs, moors, and beaches. Two bike paths lead to the eastern and western points on the island. I prefer the longer loop (23 miles), which goes past cranberry bogs and moors to the charming town of Siasconset, which locals refer to as 'Sconset.

From Steamboat Wharf in Nantucket town, turn left on South Water Street and right on Main Street. You'll have to walk your bike here since the roads are old cobblestone. A left onto Orange Street will bring you past former whaling captains' homes to a traffic rotary. Take another left around the circle onto the Milestone Road bike path. This 6-mile trail is a straight line through the heart and heath of the island to the town of **'Sconset.** Quaint rose-trellised cottages with names like The Snuggery and Very Snug line the small streets. These former fishing shacks (with low ceilings that look snug) are still used as summer homes by residents of Nantucket town.

After the bike path ends, the road continues to a rotary where you can take a right onto Ocean Beach for views of the Atlantic, and where you can lock up your bike and head down to the beach. The route continues on Broadway to Sankaty Avenue. A left at the next main intersection and a right on Wauwinet Road will bring you to my favorite village on the island, Wauwinet. I usually splurge for lunch at the **Wauwinet Inn** ($20 to $25 per person; I figure it's my reward for getting here). The innovative cuisine and the intimate setting overlooking the manicured lawns and harbor make it hard to get back on the bike. But now you'll have the energy to head back down Wauwinet Road and take a right onto Polpis. Then, 4.5 miles later, take a right onto Milestone Road and another right at the traffic rotary to Orange Street. This will bring you back to the cobblestone streets of Nantucket town.

Young's Bicycle Shop (508-228-1151), just off the ferry on Steamboat Wharf, rents bikes.

Province Lands, at Provincetown. *Distance:* 8 miles (loop). *Time:* 1 hour. *Difficulty:* Moderate. *Directions:* Take Route 6 north to the end. Look for signs for Herring Cove Beach. Park at the end of the lot.

If I lived in Provincetown, my daily workout would be a ride on the Province Lands Bike Path. The trail is anything but flat: Rollercoaster hills dip in and out of sand dunes, weaving through scrub pine forests and beaches in one of the most unusual bike paths I've ever been on. Just before sunset is the ideal time to take this ride.

From the back of Herring Cove Beach, start pedaling. At the fork, take a left and head around Great Pond. (Cape Codders and the Islanders tend to use the word Great far too often in naming locations. What's wrong with other superlatives: Spectacular Pond, or Superb Pond? Or, in keeping with New England understatement, Fine Pond?) Anyway, travel around Great Pond to Beech Forest, where the 1-mile **Beech Forest Trail** offers a worthwhile walk. Lock up your bike and stroll among the beeches and birds around a small pond.

The best part of the bike trail is next: a sweeping downhill run to the Province Lands Visitor Center. Stop and look at the mounds of sand as they fade into the ocean. Then continue on to **Race Point Beach,** which is the only spot in New England where you can watch the sun set over the Atlantic. The path continues around the loop and catches up with the main trail back to Herring Cove Beach.

Cape Cod Rail Trail. *Distance:* 50 miles (round-trip). *Time:* 3 to 6 hours. *Difficulty:* Easy. *Directions to the northern starting point:* Take Route 6 North to South Wellfleet and turn right on Lecount Hollow Road; the trail begins behind the general store. *Directions to the southern starting point:* In South Dennis, take Route 6 to Route 134 South until you see signs for the trail and parking lot. (There are also numerous places to start along the trail.)

The Cape Cod Rail Trail is one of New England's longest and most popular bike paths. Built on the former bed of the Penn Central Railroad, the trail is relatively flat and straight. On weekends in summer, you have to contend with dogs, clumsy in-line skaters, young families, and bikers who whip by you on their way to becoming the next Lance Armstrong. Yet if you want to venture away from the coast and see some of the Cape's countryside without having to deal with motorized traffic, this is one of the few ways to do it.

The trail starts in South Wellfleet on Lecount Hollow Road or in South Dennis on Route 134, depending on which direction you want to ride. Beginning in South Wellfleet, the path cruises by purple wildflowers, flowering dogwood, and small maples where red-winged blackbirds and goldfinches nest. At the Cape Cod National Seashore Visitors Center in Salt Pond, you can veer off the Cape Cod Rail Trail for 2 miles on another rolling bike trail to the dunes of **Coast Guard and Nauset Light Beaches.** Visit the candy-striped lighthouse and turn around.

In Orleans, you have to ride on Rock Harbor Road and West Road until the city council decides to complete the trail. At least you get a good view of the boats lining Rock Harbor. Clearly marked signs lead back to the Rail Trail, where you'll soon enter **Nickerson State Park.** Here you can give your legs a rest and go canoeing on Flax Pond, veer off onto 8 miles of old Nickerson State Park bike trails, or continue straight through Brewster to a series of swimming holes: Seymour, Long, and Hinckleys Ponds. A favorite picnic spot is the **Pleasant Lake General Store** in Harwich. Shortly afterward, you cross over Route 6 on Route 124 before veering right through farmland, soon ending in South Dennis.

Idle Times Bike Shop (Route 6, North Eastham; 508-255-8281) and **Rail Trail Bike and Blade** (302 Underpass Road, Brewster; 508-

896-8200) are two of the many bike rental shops that line the Rail Trail.

Cape Cod Canal Trail. *Distance:* 14 miles (round-trip). *Time:* 1 to 2 hours. *Difficulty:* Easy. *Directions:* Cross over the Bourne Bridge onto the Cape and turn right at the traffic rotary. Your next right heads downhill to a road going under the bridge. Turn right and then take a left into the parking lot.

If you like water, you'll enjoy this easy bike trail along the Cape Cod Canal. You can follow the current out to sea as you bike under the large spans of both Bourne and Sagamore Bridges. Anglers laze on the large rocks that line the trail and fish for stripers. Other fishermen, aboard their boats, cruise this wide canal that connects Buzzards Bay with Cape Cod Bay.

The paved trail is not only popular with bikers, but also with joggers, in-line skaters, walkers, and strollers, so try to avoid venturing here in peak hours. When the trail ends, continue around the Sandwich Recreation Area in the parking lot and turn left onto Moffet Road. You'll pass the Coast Guard station and proceed past a gate onto a dirt trail. This leads to a small beach and a long rock jetty that extends into Cape Cod Bay. After your fair share of serenity, simply return the way you came.

Walks and Rambles

Among the highlights of New England are the strolls on Cape Cod. Forest and moor combine with coastal marsh and sand to create the best of both worlds. The splendid bird-watching on these walks is an added bonus.

John Wing Trail/South Trail, at Brewster. *Distance:* 2.25 miles (round-trip). *Time:* 1.5 to 2 hours. *Difficulty:* Easy. *Directions:* From

Brewster, follow Route 6A west toward Dennis. The Cape Cod Museum of Natural History is located on the right, 1.6 miles from the Dennis/ Brewster line. Park in the museum's parking lot.

These two relatively flat trails that start from the Cape Cod Museum of Natural History are ideal for young families and avid bird-watchers. The South Trail is a three-quarter-mile-long path that passes through marshes and over a creek before looping around a small beech forest back to the main trail. Young osprey are often found nesting on the power-line poles here.

Across the street, in the back of the museum, the longer John Wing Trail winds through more marshlands to the beaches of Cape Cod Bay. Once you cross over the dunes, take a right and walk along the sand until you see another trail leading back to a forest of oaks and pines. A right turn at the John Wing Memorial sign leads you past the site where this European settler built a house in 1656. Take a left to reach the main trail that goes back to the museum.

Fort Hill Trail, near Eastham. *Distance:* 2 miles (round-trip). *Time:* 1 hour. *Difficulty:* Easy. *Directions:* Take Route 6 North for 1.5 miles past the Eastham–Orleans traffic rotary. A small red sign will tell you where to take a right turn to the trail. Park at the lower lot. A map is available from the Cape Cod National Seashore Visitors Center at Salt Pond.

Marshes, forests, and swamps merge with deep-rooted history and outlandish architecture to make the Fort Hill Trail one of the most magical walks on the Cape. From the parking lot, cross the street, walking under a whalebone gateway to get a good look at **Captain Edward Penniman's dream home.** In the mid-19th century, Penniman climbed the whaling ranks, from harpooner to captain, amassing a fortune in the process. He circled the globe seven times, scouring the ocean for its

Captain Edward Penniman's dream home

most lucrative products: whale oil, spermaceti, baleen, and ivory. He returned home in 1867 and proceeded to build this house in the Second French Empire Style.

The walk continues around the back of the house, where foxes and jackrabbits are often seen. After you ascend a short hill to the second parking lot, sweeping views of Nauset Marsh and the long stretches of sand known as Nauset Beach open up. This is all part of the vast Cape Cod National Seashore. In 1605, explorer Samuel de Champlain arrived on a tiny vessel to chart this area for a new French settlement. However, the shallowness of the harbor and the less than amicable welcome by the Nauset Indians forced Champlain to look elsewhere, and it wasn't until 1644 that the first colonists settled here.

The trail continues through a section of red cedar trees before arriving at an overlook called **Skiff Hill.** This is a prime location for birdwatchers to spot the great blue, green, and black-crowned night herons feasting on the marsh. Several hundred yards later, take a left at the **Red Maple Swamp Trail** onto a winding boardwalk through a murky swamp of tall red maples. A right turn at the end of the swamp will bring you back to your car.

Wellfleet Bay Wildlife Sanctuary, at Wellfleet. *Distance:* 1.5 miles (round-trip). *Time:* 1 to 2 hours. *Difficulty:* Easy. *Directions:* Heading north on Route 6, the clearly marked sign is located 0.3 mile past the Eastham/Wellfleet town line at the southern end of Wellfleet.

A chorus of chirping birds will inevitably greet you at the entrance to the Wellfleet Bay Wildlife Sanctuary. They might be white-crowned sparrows with a crown of white adorning their heads, red-winged blackbirds, even the rare orange and brown rufous-sided towhees. Yet this is only a small fraction of the birdlife found on the sanctuary's splendid trails. The Massachusetts Audubon Society, which owns and maintains the property, has reported more than 250 different species.

The **Goose Pond Trail** is a leisurely ramble though marsh, forest, ponds, and fields. At low tide, take a right at the cabin and continue on the **Try Island Trail** to a boardwalk that leads to Cape Cod Bay. On the marshes and beaches surrounding the trails, green herons and large gooselike brants are prevalent. Retrace your steps back to the cabin and continue on the Goose Pond Trail through a field to Goose Pond. The first bench overlooking the pond is one of the most serene spots on the Cape. Northern hummingbirds fly in and out of the branches overhead, forming a choir whose voices will soothe anyone's soul.

Pamet Cranberry Bog Trail, at Truro. *Distance:* 1 mile. *Time:* 1 hour. *Difficulty:* Easy. *Directions:* Take Route 6 to North Pamet Road, Truro, and park at the Environmental Education Center (a youth hostel in the summer) at the end of the road.

The Pamet Cranberry Bog Trail is a short hike around a pond to an abandoned bog house that was once used to cultivate cranberries. Take the dirt path to the right of the house, and the bucolic countryside quickly transforms to some of the most majestic and secluded beach scenery on the Cape. The path leads to the edge of the moors over-looking Truro's Ballston Beach. On a clear summer day, you'll find an occasional surfer battling the waves. Continue along the main trail to the left for even better views and the freshest sea air your deprived lungs can handle. If I was an artist and wanted to paint the Cape Cod coast, this is the spot I'd choose.

Cedar Tree Neck Sanctuary, Martha's Vineyard. *Distance:* 2.5 miles (loop). *Time:* 1 to 2 hours. *Difficulty:* Easy. *Directions:* From Vineyard Haven, take State Road south toward West Tisbury. At Indian Hill Road, take a right and follow the signs to the sanctuary. Take a right at the dirt road known as Obed Daggett and watch out for large pot-holes.

The varied Vineyard landscape is best seen on a ramble through Cedar Tree Neck Sanctuary. Forest of oaks, beeches, and sassafras trees lead to serene ponds, swampy bogs, and rocky coastline before combining all three elements in a scenic overlook.

Start at the White Trail, just to the left of the trail map signboard, and continue through the forest until you reach the second branch of the Yellow Trail. Take a right and pass under the maples and yellow beeches before stopping at **Ames Pond,** one of the most peaceful spots on the island. Birds sing overhead, butterflies play hide-and-seek, and frogs trill from sunken logs.

Walk along the edge of the pond and you'll meet up with the White Trail again. This leads to a swampy area known as a sphagnum bog, where tree roots jut out from carpets of velvety green moss. Soon you'll reach the white sands of the seashore, with views of the Elizabeth Islands across Vineyard Sound. This beach lies on the western part of the Vineyard, ideal for a sunset stroll, except for one problem: For some reason, the sanctuary closes at 5:30 PM, not dusk.

Take a right between two rows of roped fences where dune restoration work is being done and you'll skirt around **Cedar Tree Neck Pond,** once an operating cranberry bog. When the Red Trail forks, go left for a great vista of all the diverse terrain you've just encountered—forest, ponds, beach, and ocean. This is the perfect ending to an enchanting loop.

Gay Head Cliffs, Martha's Vineyard. *Distance:* 1 to 3 miles (round-trip). *Time:* 2 hours. *Difficulty:* Easy. *Directions:* The Gay Head Cliffs are at the southwestern corner of the island. Simply take State Road all the way south to where it ends at a parking loop. Parking is at the town-owned lot at the corner of State Road and Moshup Trail. The fee is $10 in the summer, and the trail starts directly behind the lot.

Gay Head Cliffs is justifiably one of the most popular spots on the island. Layers of clay create varying degrees of vivid color, depending on the sedimentary deposit. The result is a dramatic backdrop of rose-colored reds, frog greens, Van Gogh yellows, and whites along the faces of the jagged cliffs. Come summer, Gay Head Beach below the cliffs is swarming with suntanners. So come early or, even better, during sunset when the sun's rays create a spectacular light show across the clay. You might even find several seashells in mint condition to add to your collection.

The trail starts from the parking lot, winding through the brush alongside Moshup Trail, before ending at the beach. Turn right and you'll notice that the rounded cliffs become more jagged as they gain in height. You can walk along the beach as far as the surf will let you, but the closer you get to the taller cliffs, the more striking the clay becomes. For many years, nude bathers covered themselves in red clay before jumping in the ocean to supposedly smooth their skin. Sunbathing au naturel remains, but any use of the clay is now prohibited, so I guess we'll have to resort to paying for mud baths at expensive spas.

Sanford Farm and The Woods, Nantucket. *Distance:* 4 miles (round-trip). *Time:* 1.5 to 2 hours. *Difficulty:* Easy. *Directions:* From Nantucket town, take Madaket Road 2 miles west. The parking lot is clearly marked on the left side of the road.

Sanford Farm's pastoral setting is well worth the detour from the beach. This is the Nantucket of yore, far away from the million-dollar mansions of today. Indeed, **Sanford Farm** was Nantucket's first settlement, with colonists who were happy just to have a roof over their head and enough sustenance to survive. Enter through a turnstile onto a dirt road that passes fields of wildflowers and a freshwater marsh, **Trots Swamp.** The trail continues past two wooden posts that once marked the boundary of an area called **The Woods.** Winterberry, blackberry, and bayberry shrubs line both sides of the path and are home to white-tailed deer and cottontail rabbits (which you'll undoubtedly see).

Another 15-minute stroll and you'll end up at a vacated barn that sits in the center of a large clearing. Resplendent views of Hummock Pond to the left, the town of Madaket to the right, and the Atlantic Ocean open before you. The trail continues to the ocean and an area called Ram's Pasture. However, I usually sit on the bench, in the clearing, take in the countryside, and then retrace my steps back to plaque #7. A right turn here takes you on a quick loop around a small pond that offers some of the best bird-watching on the island. Red-tailed hawks and osprey usually hover above. Take a right at the end of the loop to return to the lot.

TWO, IF BY SEA

Canoeing

If you own your own canoe or kayak, **Barnstable Harbor** is a fun place to spend several hours gliding through the marsh. This is especially true on Wednesdays or weekends when clammers are digging for their weekly bucket of littleneck steamers. The harbor is a long inlet on the southern shores of Sandy Neck Beach. The best time to paddle is high tide, before the water level drops dramatically. To get there from Yarmouth, take Route 6A west past Barnstable. Take a right on Scudder Lane. There's parking at the end of the road.

Nickerson State Park, Brewster. *Distance:* 1–3 miles. *Time:* 1 to 2 hours. *Difficulty:* Easy. *Directions:* Take Route 6 to exit 12 and turn onto Route 6A West. You'll reach the park entrance on the left in 1.6 miles.

The 300-plus kettle ponds found on the Cape and Islands are entirely dependent on groundwater and precipitation. There are no rivers or streams feeding these ponds. These ponds and the tributaries that run to the harbors are ideal flatwater canoeing and kayaking locales. Three of these ponds—**Cliff, Little Cliff, and Flax Ponds**—provide great paddling in Nickerson State Park. They have sandy shores, but you might have to drag your canoe out a short way if the water level is low.

From the western shores of Cliff Pond, off Nook Road, you can paddle around the circular body of water, nestled in a forest of pitch pine, oak, and hemlock trees. The pond is stocked yearly with trout and bass, just in case you want to exchange paddle for pole.

Tisbury Great Pond

Jack's Boat Rentals (508-896-8556) rents canoes at Nickerson State Park.

Tisbury Great Pond, Martha's Vineyard. *Distance:* 1 to 3 miles. *Time:* 1 to 2 hours. *Difficulty:* Easy. *Directions:* From West Tisbury, take West Tisbury Road toward Edgartown. Turn right at Tiah's Cove Road and another right on Clam Point Road. The parking is located on the right. For maps, contact the Vineyard Land Bank Commission (508-627-7141). (The Great Pond is part of Sepiessa Point Reservation on the Land Bank maps.)

The ponds, lagoons, and coastline on Martha's Vineyard are ideal for flatwater kayaking or canoeing. Most noted are Edgartown Great Pond, Lake Tashmoo, Poucha Pond in Chappaquiddick, Squibnocket Pond in Gay Head, and this trip to Tisbury Great Pond. **The Trustees of Reservations** (508-693-7662; www.thetrustees.org) offers natural-history canoe tours on Poucha Pond; they last two hours and cost $25.

Tiah's Cove is one of the fingers that form inlets into Tisbury Great Pond. The cove is part of the Vineyard's Land Bank: conservation lands that were bought by the island after a 2 percent Land Bank tax was added to all real estate transactions beginning in 1986. The law has resulted in preservation of thousands of acres of environmentally sensitive habitat.

The put-in for this paddle trip is at the northeastern part of **Tiah's Cove** near the small parking lot. Even with a strong wind, you can paddle the whole length of the cove into Great Pond before turning back. On a clear day, you can paddle to Quansoo and continue on to Black Point Pond. Bring your shucking knife, because the pond is known for its delicious oysters. Simply reach down to pick up one of the shells on the pond floor, open it up, and you'll have one of the most succulent oysters on the half shell you've ever tasted. On the way back, try to avoid the wind by staying close to the shore. Large trumpeter swans are known to keep you company on the water.

Kayaks and canoes can be rented at **Wind's Up,** at 95 Beach Road, Vineyard Haven; 508-693-4252.

Fishing

Cape Cod and the Islands are to blues and stripers what Montana is to trout—home to a fishing frenzy. Between late July and early October, the bluefish are abundant, striking hard and fighting tirelessly. Every time you throw your line out, you'll get a bite from these insatiable eaters. Striped bass are a bit more elusive, but still very catchable. Locals start hooking "keepers" in late May and continue throughout the summer.

The best surf-casting is on the **Outer Cape,** from Nauset to Race Point. Favorite beaches include Coast Guard Beach and Race Point

Beach. The fish move farther north as the summer wears on. In July and August, crowds of suntanners scare off the fish. Thus the night or early morning hours are the best times to be out there. For bait, use poppers during the day and sand eels at night for the blues; sand eels during the day and live eels at night for stripers. All the Cape's bait and tackle shops sell them. For instruction, contact **Fishing the Cape** in East Harwich (508-432-1200). They conduct 2-day saltwater fly-fishing courses.

In **Nantucket,** surf-cast off Great Point or Sankaty Head. **Cross Rip Outfitters** (24 Easy Street, Nantucket; 508-228-4900) is a good place on the island to find gear, instruction, and guide service.

As for **Martha's Vineyard,** wherever there's water is conceivably a good place to cast. However, some of the highly recommended spots are the rip off Wasque Point in Chappaquiddick, Town Beach in Gay Head, and the beach south of the Edgartown Great Pond. For a guide, it's hard to beat Cooper Gilkes, a third-generation islander who knows all the coveted spots on the Vineyard. Coop's guided trips last four to five hours and he offers fly fishing and deep-sea fishing as well as surf-casting. You can reach him at **Coop's Bait and Tackle,** at 147 West Tisbury Road, near Edgartown; 508-627-3909.

There's elephant tuna, blue tuna, and bonita to be had when you venture offshore, but most likely you'll catch scup, tautog, fluke, sea bass, and other bottom fish. A variety of boats will get you out to the hot spots. *Hy-line* (508-790-0696) operates out of Hyannis's Ocean Street Docks. In Harwichport, the *Pauly V* (508-430-0053) comes highly recommended. In Nantucket, try the *Albacore,* at slip 17 on Straight Wharf (508-228-5074), and *Just Do It Too,* at slip 13 on Straight Wharf (508-228-7448). **North Shore Charters** (508-645-2993) operates out of Menemsha on Martha's Vineyard.

Don't overlook the freshwater fishing opportunities on the Cape.

Fishing for stripers in Cape Cod Canal

The glacial kettles are well-stocked and, in early May, when the water temperatures hit the 50s, the fish start to bite. Flycasters wade in Wellfleet's perfectly round Gull Pond to hook trout, smallmouth and largemouth bass, white perch, and pickerel. The pond is located a mile east of Route 6 on Gull Pond Road. The brown trout at Barnstable's Lovells Pond grow to robust size. At Nickerson State Park's Cliff Pond, a boat launch lets you get out on the water to troll slowly past schools of feisty rainbows and browns. The smaller Flax and Little Cliff Ponds are good for wading.

Sailing

With numerous coves and protected harbors on the nearby Elizabeth Islands, and a strong southwesterly wind blowing 15 knots almost every afternoon, Cape sailing is considered some of the finest on the East Coast. The waters are inundated with yachts, Hobie cats, Sunfish, schooners, even the 6-foot-2 dinghy known as the Cape Cod Frosty. The Elizabeth Islands start off Woods Hole and run to the south. Only Cuttyhunk, the outermost island, and Penikese, a former leper colony—now a state-owned bird refuge and site of a school for troubled boys—remain public. The two most popular anchorages are Hadley Harbor and Tarpaulin Cove on the north and south sides, respectively, of privately owned Naushon Island. The Forbes family, which owns the island, allows sailors on the beach, but not inland. Tarpaulin Cove is a half-mile-long stretch of water with small oak trees lining the beach. Other favorite sailing destinations around the Cape include Monomoy Island at the Cape's elbow, near Chatham.

Boat rentals are widely available. **Flyer's** in Provincetown (131A Commercial Street; 508-487-0898) rents a variety of vessels from a 27-foot Irwin down to Sunfish and Hobie cats.

On Martha's Vineyard, **When and If Charters** in Vineyard Haven (508-693-4658) rents a 63-foot crewed sailboat by the day or week. **Wind's Up** (95 Beach Road, Vineyard Haven; 508-693-4252) rents Sunfish and catamarans.

On Nantucket, **Nantucket Harbor Sail** at Swains Wharf (508-228-0424) offers Rhodes 19-footers for the half-day or day. **Force 5 Watersports** (508-228-0700) rents Sunfish from Jetties Beach.

Scuba Diving

East Coast Divers in Hyannis (508-775-1185; www.ecdivers.com) can have you certified after two weekends in a Cape Cod pond. Instruction culminates with an ocean dive. In Nantucket, divers meet in front of **Sunken Ship** (12 Broad Street; 508-228-9226) every Sunday at 7:30 AM to dive the wrecks; cost is $85.

Sea Kayaking

In line with the rest of the Atlantic coast, sea kayaking is growing in popularity on the Cape and Islands. Don't miss the opportunity to sea kayak on Cape Cod's shores. When the sun is shining and the surf is relatively calm, the sport's sublime.

Eastern Mountain Sports (1513 Iyanough Road, Hyannis; 508-362-8690) has kayak demonstrations every Saturday morning in summer. They also host guided kayak tours and offer kayaks for rent. **Off the Coast Kayak** in Provincetown (877-785-2925) features half-day guided tours around Provincetown, Truro, and Wellfleet, on the Cape Cod Bay side.

Experienced kayakers may want to try a 4-mile loop from Harding Beach around **North Monomoy Island.** Monomoy National Wildlife Refuge is known for its incredible birdlife and for the schools of harbor and gray seals awaiting your arrival (see "Birding").

Sea kayaking in and around Martha's Vineyard requires much stronger paddling. Strong sea kayakers can paddle from Martha's Vineyard and across Vineyard Sound to Tarpaulin Cove on Naushon Island in the Elizabeth Islands in a little over an hour. People have also kayaked from the Vineyard to Nantucket, but you'd better be an expert to attempt this. Rentals and instruction are available at **Wind's Up** (95 Beach Road, Vineyard Haven; 508-693-4252).

In Nantucket, you can rent sea kayaks from **Force 5 Watersports** at Jetties Beach (508-228-0700) for trips within the protected harbor to Pocomo Head.

Hyannis Harbor. *Distance:* 2–4 miles. *Time:* 2 to 3 hours. *Difficulty:* Moderate. *Directions:* From downtown Hyannis, head east on Main Street and take a right on Lewis Bay Road. Another right on Bayview Road will bring you to the Inner Harbor parking lot.

Sea kayaking Hyannis Harbor

You can go sightseeing by kayak, as proven by this jaunt around Hyannis Harbor. Put in at the Hyannis Inner Harbor. Coasting along the Inner Harbor shoreline, you'll glide by the **John F. Kennedy Memorial** before passing the jetty that leads to wide-open Nantucket Sound. Sailboats, fishing boats, and tour boats will give you the right-of-way through this narrow passage, but still be cautious.

Turn right, gliding by the numerous wind surfers off Kalmus Park Beach before continuing to **Hyannisport,** site of the famous Kennedy compound with its summer homes for members of the Kennedy family. Depending on your arm strength, you can keep on paddling around the breakwater and lighthouse to Craigville Beach, or head back.

Surfing

When hurricane swells from the Caribbean sweep up the Atlantic seaboard in summer, most people on the East Coast batten down the hatches and hide indoors. Well, everybody, that is, except surfers on the Massachusetts isle of Martha's Vineyard. The Vineyard is gaining acclaim among salty dogs as *the* place to be when tropical depressions make their move north from mid-July to mid-September. Wave height can often top 10 feet.

"We dream about that one summer storm that keeps spinning for two to three days, 150 miles offshore," says local surf bum Jon DeBlase, who doubles as chef at the French restaurant L'Etoile. DeBlase notes, however, that the surf is reasonably good year-round. In the winter, there are nor'easters, and even without inclement weather, the swells frequently reach a good three to four feet. The trick to finding good surf, notes DeBlase, is an incredible amount of patience. "When I lived in Maui, surfing was a no-brainer. You just grabbed your board and hit the waves anytime," he says. "Here, you have to wait."

DeBlase says the best time for the sport is in the early morning hours, before the winds pick up. He suggests heading to the southwestern part of the island, where the surf seems to be more consistent. Squibnocket Beach has a good-sized parking lot and locals tend to be nice to newcomers. If it's too crowded, take a 15-minute stroll to nearby Bell's Beach. Both beaches are supposedly reserved for town residents only, but that rule is rarely enforced in the wee morning hours. For a public beach, visit Moshup, at Gay Head, where the surfing has great potential on a south swell. If the Atlantic resembles a duck pond, you always have the consolation that Gay Head and its multihued clay cliffs provide the most scenic spot on the island.

Boards and wet suits can be rented at **Wind's Up** in Vineyard Haven (508-693-4252). Most surfers use thrusters, with lengths from 5-foot-3 to 6-foot-4. Longboards are also popular. The ocean temperature averages 68 degrees Fahrenheit in July and August, so a spring suit provides adequate cold protection on most days.

Surfers in Nantucket flock to Cisco and Madaket Beaches.

On Cape Cod, check out the beaches of the Outer Cape, especially

The desolate dunes of Cape Cod

White Crest Beach in South Wellfleet, Ballston Beach in Truro, and sections of Nauset Beach in Orleans. You can rent boards from **Nauset Sports** on Route 6A in Orleans (508-255-4742).

Whale Watching

The sky was blue and the sea was like a mirror the morning I boarded the *Dolphin Princess* whale-watching cruise. Less than 45 minutes into our ride, someone on the starboard side of the boat gave a shout. Everyone ran over to see a huge shadow rising from the water only 15 feet away. A small geyser shot from the animal's backside as the sound of clicking cameras reverberated around the deck. Several minutes later, the same whale's tail fin, or fluke, surfaced. Wow!

Naturalist Phil Trell, from the Center for Coastal Studies, said we had just spotted a humpback whale. Phil had given us an extensive introduction to the whales of the Northeast on the ride over to Stellwagen Bank. Located about 7 miles north of Provincetown and 25 miles east of Boston, Stellwagen Bank is an 18-mile-long crescent-shaped underwater mesa, ranging from 80 to 500 feet below the surface. Currents slam into the bank, bringing nutrient-rich cold water to the surface. This attracts fish, which in turn attract numerous species of whales from April to November: humpbacks, the larger fin whales, and the smaller minkes. One gulp from a hungry humpback can take in a ton of fish. We watched the humpback for a good hour, saw him playing with a buddy, and then returned to Provincetown. The four hours aboard the boat was time well spent.

The **Dolphin Fleet** boats leave from Provincetown Harbor daily in the morning and afternoon and at 5:00 PM for a sunset cruise; the cost is $20. The fleet's office is in the Chamber of Commerce building at the head of the pier (1-800-826-9300; www.whalewatch.com).

Wind Surfing

All a wind surfer needs is a prevailing wind and a steady diet of waves to catch some air. On Nantucket Sound, wind speeds exceeding 20 knots are the norm, not the exception, and the shallow water helps mount waves quickly. Kalmus Beach, south of Hyannis, is the board-sailing mecca, be it spring, summer, or fall. Every wind surfer on the Cape knows this, so the waters are usually covered with sails.

If the crowds get to you, try nearby West Dennis Beach, or Forest Beach (at the end of Forest Beach Road, off Route 28, in Chatham). Phil Clark, owner of **Nauset Sports** on Route 6A in Orleans (508-255-4742), is an avid wind surfer. He rents sailboards, provides instruction, and tends to give away his secret spots when coaxed.

Wind surfers sail to Pocomo Heads on Nantucket. Rentals and instruction are available from **Force 5 Watersports** at Jetties Beach (508-228-0700).

On Martha's Vineyard, rentals and lessons are available from **Wind's Up** (95 Beach Road, Vineyard Haven; 508-693-4252). You can sail behind the shop on Lagoon Pond or try the long stretch of beach between Oak Bluffs and Edgartown.

A DAY AT THE BEACH

The category you've been patiently waiting for. The envelope please...

For the most scenic stretch of sand on the Cape, it's hard to top the **Cape Cod National Seashore.** Easily accessible along Route 6, 40 miles of rolling, windswept sand dunes, kettlehole ponds, bogs, plains, scrub forest, and marshes combine to form this serene, protected land. Like most of Cape Cod, the land was coveted by developers until Congress intervened and purchased the region in 1961. Also known as the Outer Cape, this fragile barrier spit stretches from the southern tip of Nauset Beach in Orleans to Race Point Lighthouse outside of Provincetown.

The National Seashore comprises 15 beaches. Six are run by the National Park Service, the others are managed by the towns in which they lie. Everyone has their favorite beach. On **Nauset Beach,** the sand seems to stretch to the horizon and you can walk for miles along the dunes. At **Nauset Light and Coast Guard Beaches** in Eastham, the shore is sheltered by small bluffs to give it more of a wild feel. **Newcomb Hollow and Cahoon Hollow Beaches** in Wellfleet are less crowded, while **Race Point Beach** in Provincetown is the Cape Cod you've dreamed of—rolling sand dunes, open ocean, and seemingly endless shoreline. **Flyer's** (508-487-0518) in Provincetown will shuttle you to the tip of the Cape, at **Long Point Beach** (round-trip price is $10), or you can walk there in an hour. All of the National Seashore beaches have good surf and thus are ideal for boogie boarders and surfers.

Coast Guard Beach in Eastham

Cape Cod beaches on Nantucket Sound, like **West Dennis Beach** in West Dennis and **Kalmus Beach** in Hyannis, have strong winds and are favored by wind surfers.

Young families whose kids are not yet strong swimmers congregate on the calm north-facing sands of Cape Cod Bay. Here you'll find warmer waters and teeming tide pools. At low tide, you and the youngsters can venture far out into Cape Cod Bay. From Dennis to Orleans, places like **Corporation, Paine's Creek, and Skaket Beaches** are popular in summer with the pail-and-shovel crowd. Skaket is also the place for watching sunsets, but bugs can be annoying in July and August. College crowds congregate at **Craigville Beach** in Centerville and **Nauset Beach** in Orleans.

On the Vineyard, most-scenic-beach awards go to **East Beach** in Chappaquiddick and to **Moshup and Lobsterville Beaches** in Gay Head. Families head for 2-mile-long **State Beach,** between Oak Bluffs and Edgartown, and **Menemsha Beach. Katama Beach,** near Edgartown, is a serious college scene.

All of Nantucket's beaches seem to have good surf, except for the aptly named **Children's Beach** in Nantucket Harbor. Nearby **Jetties Beach** is also popular with families, with its playground, snack bar, and skateboarding park. An easy 3-mile bike trail outside Nantucket town leads to expansive **Surfside Beach,** active with the singles crowd. An up-and-down 5-mile bike path leads to the more remote **Madaket Beach** on the west point of the island. Sloping down to the sea, the beach has a wild, blustery feel to it. A longer bike trail leads to **'Sconset Beach** on the eastern point of the island. Of course, beachcombers who don't want to work up a sweat can always arrive by car.

Nude suntanning is illegal and I wouldn't want to be arrested as an accomplice, but you might try **Lucy Vincent Beach** in Gay Head,

Miacomet Beach in Nantucket, and the remote corners of **Longnook Beach** in Truro.

CAMPGROUNDS

Public campgrounds are listed first, then private.

Nickerson State Park, Brewster (508-896-3491). From the junction of Route 6 and Route 6A, head 1.6 miles west on Route 6A. The park provides 420 sites (no hook-ups), handicapped-accessible rest rooms, hot showers, flush toilets, and grills. The well-spaced sites are in extremely high demand during the summer. If you're one of the fortunate few to grab one, have fun exploring the hiking and biking trails that weave through the park's ponds and woods.

Shawne Crowell State Forest, Sandwich (508-888-0351). From Sandwich, head 1.5 miles north on Route 6A and then 1.5 miles on Route 130. The facility offers 280 sites (no hook-ups), handicapped-accessible rest rooms, hot showers, flush toilets, and grills. After Nickerson State Park, this rates as the second-best state-operated campground. The campgrounds are located near the historic village of Sandwich.

Peters Pond Park, Sandwich (508-477-1775). After driving over the Sagamore Bridge, continue on Route 6 to exit 2. Turn right onto Route 130 and travel 3 miles to Quaker Meeting House Road. Turn left and then turn right at the next set of lights onto Cotuit Road. The campground is half a mile ahead on the right. The park has 500 sites (278 with full hook-ups; 100 with water and electric), metered hot showers, rest rooms, laundry, a grocery store, ice, a playground, and a recreation hall. Peters Pond Park is on a mile-long stretch of beach, offering swimming and bass and trout fishing. Sites are in a shaded forest, never far from the salty sea air.

Paine's Campground, Wellfleet (508-349-3007). At the junction of Route 6 and Old County Road in Wellfleet (1 mile north of Marconi Beach), turn right (east) onto Old County Road. Three-quarters of a mile later, you'll see the campground. Here are 150 sites (25 with hook-ups), picnic tables, metered hot showers, ice, and grills. A mere mile from the dunes of Marconi Beach, Paine's Campground provides specialized areas for families, singles, and couples. Hiking and biking trails lead to the Cape Cod National Seashore.

Horton's Camping Resort, Truro (508-487-1220). From Route 6 in North Truro, take South Highland Road east for 1 mile to the campground. The resort features 222 sites (76 with hook-ups), picnic tables, metered showers, flush toilets, laundry, a snack bar, and a playground. At Horton's, a scrub pine forest is all that separates your tent from the Atlantic Ocean. A path leads to the century-old Highland Golf Links course and the Highland Light.

Dunes' Edge Campground, Provincetown (508-487-9815). Travel 2 miles past the "Entering Provincetown" sign and turn right at mile marker 116. The campground is on your right. There are 100 sites (22 with hook-ups), hot showers, laundry, and a small grocery store. Dunes' Edge is an apt name for this campground on the edge of Cape Cod National Seashore. You can walk to Race Point Beach from the wooded sites or bike the Province Lands Bike Path.

Webb's Camping Area, Martha's Vineyard (508-693-0233). From the Oak Bluff ferry, go 0.25 mile west on Oak Bluff Road, 0.5 mile southwest on Circuit Road, and 1.5 miles southwest on Barnes Road. You'll find 166 sites (140 without hook-ups; 26 with water and electricity), group sites for tents, hot showers, flush toilets, laundry, a grocery store, ice, picnic tables, and grills. Sites are in a secluded pine forest overlooking Lagoon Pond.

Nantucket has no camping facilities.

CHAPTER FOUR

Massachusetts:
Boston, the North Shore, and the South Shore

▶ Consider the history of this region and you'll realize that it runs concurrently with the history of American sports. The first sailors were the Pilgrims who, on December 8, 1620, sailed into Plymouth Bay in a snowstorm. They soon became the first walkers on the new land when on December 11, William Bradford reported that a small party of Pilgrims "marched into the land and found diverse cornfields and little running brooks, a place fit for the situation." Unfortunately, these hard-core adventurers were also the nation's first campers. Living in lean-tos they dug in the ground, less than half the Pilgrims survived their first winter.

In time, the Pilgrims prospered and communities spread north to Boston, Salem, and the fishing communities of Gloucester and Marblehead. By the mid-1630s, immigrants, chiefly Puritans, were coming to the coast of Massachusetts at a rate of two thousand a year. They entered a land devoid of trees. As William Cronon noted in his book *Changes in the Land,* "Boston was nearly barren and colonists were forced to seek wood from nearby islands." But it became the perfect place for urban development. By 1700, the population of the Massachusetts Bay region had swelled to over 100,000.

Remarkably, Boston never became a sprawling metropolis like its neighbor to the south. Today, you can drive 20 minutes from the city center and be at Concord's Walden Pond. A 30-minute drive will take you to Carlisle and the rural communities of the northwest. An hour north and you can be on the soft sands of Cape Ann or Plum Island. An hour from the center of Manhattan, on the other hand, still leaves you in the suburbs, or perhaps battling traffic in the Holland Tunnel. That's not to say Boston doesn't have its share of traffic problems. Traveling south on I-93 from the city on The Artery is a nightmare, especially during rush hour. Now that construction is ongoing to expand the number of lanes, you can expect delays southbound for the next five years. Regardless, Boston is the hub of New England and the usual starting point for a vacation in the region.

Head outdoors here and you'll almost always be accompanied by the origins of American history. Bike around Cape Ann through Gloucester, the oldest fishing community in the nation, and Rocky Neck, the oldest continuing art colony in the country. Canoe on the Concord River under Old North Bridge to see the spot where the first battle of the Revolutionary War took place. Walk on World's End, one of the last in Massachusetts Bay of those glacier-born hills known as drumlins. And then there's the sea that brought the Pilgrims here. Both the North Shore—the coastline north of Boston—and the South Shore offer a variety of beaching opportunities, from mile-long stretches of sand to intimate coves. Several outfitters arrange sea kayaking trips, one of which visits the humpback whales at Stellwagen Bank. Run into one of these massive mammals in a small plastic boat and you might just get a sense of how it felt to be on the *Mayflower* for its perilous nine-week journey across the Atlantic.

THE TERRAIN

Drumlins and the fields of boulders known as boulder trains predominate in the 30- to 50-mile-wide coastal plains of eastern Massachusetts. Drumlins are smooth, gentle hills no more than 200 feet high that are essentially piles of glacial till—an infertile mixture of clay, gravel, and sand. They have no core of bedrock. At one time, more than 50 of these oval-shaped mounds were located in or around low-lying Massachusetts Bay. The best-known example is Bunker Hill, site of the Revolutionary War battle. Over the years, the number of drumlins have diminished due to the continuous battering of waves and ongoing urban development. Waters from the Atlantic have washed away many of the islands in Boston Harbor, including 12-acre Nix's Mate. All that remains of this drumlin is a small shoal. Real estate development has camouflaged other hills, making it hard to recognize the shape under sprawling highways and houses. One of the finest examples of a drumlin today is World's End, just north of Hingham (see "Walks and Rambles").

Similar to Narragansett Basin in Rhode Island, the low relief of Boston Basin is known for its soft clay and coal deposits. Bedrock is much more evident in the Cape Ann area. The ancient retreating ice cap split the bedrock into large boulders that are now strewn along the rugged shores. This is best seen on the coast of Halibut Point State Park (see "Walks and Rambles"). Inland, eastern Massachusetts has many state forests and reservations where oaks, hickories, and maples thrive.

GETTING HERE

From **Boston**, I-95 and Route 1 head north from the city, where Route 128 veers off I-95 to the **North Shore** and Cape Ann. Route 128 and I-95 also form a beltway around the suburbs of Boston. To head to the

South Shore, take I-93 south from Boston to Route 3, which is the gateway to all the beaches on the way to Sagamore Bridge and Cape Cod. You can reach Horseneck Beach, Westport, and South Dartmouth via Route 24 off I-93. Most of the activities in this chapter will center first on the Boston area and then branch out to cover the nearby North Coast and then the more extended South Coast.

Cruising around a traffic rotary without cutting off too many cars is Boston's version of a scenic drive. Outside the city, Route 114 to Marblehead, Plum Island Road, and Route 127 around Cape Ann are picturesque drives. In October, the bogs that line Route 58 in Plympton near Plymouth are red with cranberries.

The Activities

ONE, IF BY LAND

Ballooning

Gary and Ken Lovell take passengers on sunrise adventures over the South Shore. Call **Balloons over New England** at 1-800-788-5562.

Birding

You don't have to travel far from Boston to find excellent birding. **Great Meadows National Wildlife Refuge** is only 20 minutes away in Concord (Wier Hill Road; 978-465-5753), just west of the city. Located on the shores of the Concord and Sudbury Rivers, this 3,600-acre freshwater wetland is home to a large number of migratory birds. Glossy ibises, snowy egrets, great blue herons, and yellow warblers are some of the more than 200 species that have been recorded here in the past 10 years. Canoeing offers entrance to some of the least-visited marshes, or simply walk the loop (see "Walks and Rambles"). Two large constructed ponds full of cattails are the highlight. Depending on water level, if mud is exposed, expect to find American and least bitterns, wood ducks, marsh wrens, and herons.

If you're in Boston and you don't have a lot of time, check out the **Mt. Auburn Cemetery** (580 Mt. Auburn Street) in Cambridge. In May and June, the front gate is unlocked at 6 AM. Simply enter and treat yourself to a wake-up call of warblers, tanagers, and orioles. Opened in 1831 by the Massachusetts Horticultural Society, Mt. Auburn is America's first garden cemetery. Today, Mt. Auburn is an urban oasis of 600 types of trees and 50,000 annuals. Call the Mt. Auburn bird line during migration (617-547-7105, ext. 824). The **Brookline Bird Club** (617-547-7105; www.massbird.org) runs daily bird walks here in May and June, meeting at the front gate at 6 AM.

Perhaps the finest viewing in the region occurs at the **Parker River National Wildlife Refuge** on Plum Island (261 Northern Blvd.; 978-465-5753) The northern third of this 8-mile-long barrier island 30 miles north of Boston is developed. The remainder consists of the 4,662-acre refuge. Wander through the barrier beach, thickets, and salt marshes to view up to 350 bird species. Beaches on the refuge are closed during the prime sunning months of June, July, and August so that the short, stocky endangered piping plovers can nest undisturbed. Although the beach is off-limits then, the thickets and marsh are still an excellent area to spot migrating shorebirds like black-bellied plovers, short-billed dowitchers, warblers, sandpipers, and godwits. The boardwalk on the Hellcat Swamp Trail circles around the murky grasses to an observation tower and blind. Pull into parking lot no. 4 to start the trail. At the salt pans, spend time scanning for hawks, egrets, and herons. Plum Island is located on the North Shore, 4 miles from Route 1, near Newburyport.

In spring and fall, also on the North Shore, check out the small wildlife sanctuary of **Marblehead Neck** (Risley Road, Marblehead), run by the Massachusetts Audubon Society (1-800-283-8266). Several trails lead from the parking lot to a pond and up a short hill where birders come to gaze at warblers, thrushes, and orioles.

An Audubon-run spot on the South Shore is the **Daniel Webster Sanctuary,** in Marshfield. Take Cemetery Road to the end and park. A trail leads to a small hill where you have good views of meadows and marsh. This is a favorite hunting ground for hawks and owls. Also be on the lookout for waterfowl and shorebirds.

On the southwestern shores in South Dartmouth, **Allens Pond Wildlife Refuge** features 300 acres of undeveloped barrier beaches, dunes, and coastal heathlands. It's located on the southern tip of Horseneck Road, just before East Beach.

For information on walking tours at **Massachusetts Audubon Society** properties, call 1-800-283-8266 or visit www.massaudubon.org.

Golf

There's nothing like getting out on a golf course, smelling the sweet, freshly mowed grass, hearing your spikes squeak as you follow that perfectly struck ball rising, then falling onto the green, maybe even sinking a 15-foot putt. Unlike tennis courts, no two golf courses are alike and thus, even if your game is off, you can at least savor the scenery.

In the Boston area, private clubs like Braeburn in Cambridge, the Salem Country Club, and The Country Club in Brookline have a 10- to 20-year waiting list to join. That's because there's a limited number of marquee public courses in the region.

Shaker Hills in Harvard (508-772-2227) boasts a quintessential Massachusetts design cut of forest and old rock walls. Pro Eric

Kohberger offers six one-hour lessons for $450. **Stow Acres** in Stow (978-568-1100) also boasts a stellar reputation, which often means long waits for tee times and crowded weekends in summer. For good instruction closer to Boston, the **Newton Commonwealth Golf Course** (617-630-1971), near the Boston College campus, is one of the easier course designs in the area. Four half-hour lessons cost $160.

On the South Shore is **Widow's Walk** in Scituate Harbor (781-544-7777). One of the forerunners toward the trend of environmentally correct golf, this former garbage dump was transformed into an exquisite course. The signature hole, the par-3 17th, is elevated, with good views of the North River and the Atlantic in the distance. There's also the **Presidents Golf Course** in Quincy (617-328-3444), the state's only county-owned course. In Plymouth, **Marriott** (508-209-9000) has just built a new hotel and conference center that features four golf courses; two were designed by Rees Jones and another by Jack Nicklaus.

The North Shore contains almost exclusively private country clubs, with no recommended public courses.

Horseback Riding

The trails at **Blue Hills Reservation Area** keep Boston riders happy. Call Blue Hills (617-698-1802) for a list of local stables. On the South Shore, **Briggs Riding Stables** (781-826-3191) in Hanover offers private and group lessons as well as trail rides. **Bobby's Ranch** (978-263-7165) in Westford offers guided rides in the North Shore for novice to expert; with 2,000 acres, the ranch provides plenty of room to roam.

Mountain Biking

Head to any of the state forests, parks, and reservations of eastern Massachusetts and you'll find a vast web of trails to get lost on. This includes local favorites like the 3,500-acre **Wompatuck State Park** in Hingham, where dirt road and doubletrack rides are plentiful, **Ames Norwell State Park** in Abington, and **Gilbert Hills State Forest** in Foxboro.

Then there's more coveted riding that only a Boston suburbanite would know about. The 2,000-acre **Middlesex Fells Reservation** in Winchester features a dandy 7-mile loop around three reservoirs. **Noanet Woodlands** in Dover has 5 miles of trails that weave through much-needed forest. Then there's the **Lynn Woods** in Lynn, a 2,200-acre reservation where you'll be treated to great vistas along man-made lakes.

The following rides are my personal favorites.

Blue Hills State Reservation. *Distance:* Varies. *Time:* Your call. *Difficulty:* Moderate. *Directions:* From the junction of I-93 and Route 28 (exit 5), drive 1.4 miles north on Route 28 and turn right onto Chickatawbut Road. There's a small gravel lot for parking on your right.

Boston's favorite place to mountain bike is this 6,000-acre reservation just south of the city. Park your car and cruise up the dirt road known as the Braintree Pass Path. Branching off the road are numerous singletrack and doubletrack routes including the Skyline. Blue-blazed, rock-littered Skyline cruises up Chickatawbut Hill, rising up and down, before descending past Blue Hills Reservoir. The major downfall of this challenging ride is that traffic from I-93 can often be heard. When you reach the layers of granite known as The Crags, you can attempt to take the Crags Foot Path or simply retrace your route on the Skyline back to the parking lot.

Maudslay State Park. *Distance:* 6 miles (loop). *Time:* 1 hour. *Difficulty:* Easy. *Directions:* From Boston and all other points south, take exit 57 off I-95 toward Newburyport and turn right on Route 113.

After 0.4 mile, turn left onto Noble Street. When the road ends, veer left and look for signs to the park.

Purchased by the state in 1985, the site of Maudslay State Park is a former estate where annual literary festivals were held in the 1850s and 1860s. Ralph Waldo Emerson, John Greenleaf Whittier, and William Lloyd Garrison were just a few of the noted writers who gathered on this 20-acre stretch of the Merrimack River to compete in one of the country's first poetry slams.

Mountain laurel, azalea, rhododendron, and flowering dogwood line the carriage-path trails that loop around the property. For the budding biker who doesn't have time to hit the trails at Acadia National Park, this easy loop is an excellent alternative. From the parking lot, cross the large field and continue to bear right on the pine needle–covered paths the entire way. The singletrack hiking trails are strictly off-limits to bikes. After a short cruise in the woods, you'll soon hug the shores of the mighty Merrimack. The trail cruises up a short hill to the remains of the estate's formal gardens before veering right to the parking lot.

Willowdale State Forest. *Distance:* varies. *Time:* As long as you'd like. *Difficulty:* Easy to moderate. *Directions:* From Ipswich, take Route 133 West, where you turn left onto Linebrook Road. Take another left onto Old Right Road and you'll see a small pullover on the left just before the road turns to gravel.

If you want to go mountain biking on the North Shore, Willowdale State Forest is one of the better choices. Former logging roads, doubletracks, and singletracks snake through the deep, dark oak and pine forest. Cruise toward the unpaved road and take a left past the gate a hundred yards later. The road curves around a farm for a quick dose of sunshine before heading back into the forest. Here, a singletrack leads into the woods, where the only sounds you hear are the ruffling of chipmunks scurrying through the leaves. An hour later, you'll make it back to the pavement of Linebrook Road.

Road Biking

Boston takes its biking very seriously. When I lived in Cambridge, there were four bike shops within three blocks of my apartment. Just on Massachusetts Avenue, I saw bikers with suits going to work, bikers with backpacks heading to school, and crazed riders who seemed to enjoy weaving in and out of the traffic.

Boston has two bike paths where you can escape the traffic and get a workout. The 10.5-mile **Minute Man Bikeway** starts in Somerville, near Davis Square, and swings by a football field, the Alewife MBTA Red Line Station, and the white swans of Spy Pond before connecting with the Arlington portion of the ride. From here, the paved trail follows a former Boston and Maine Railroad line behind homes, factories, and warehouses. When you get closer to Lexington, fields of wildflowers and small playgrounds replace the real estate. The trail ends in the village of Bedford. All along the path are places to rent and repair bikes and get cold drinks.

The 17.1-mile **Charles River Bike Path** runs from the Museum of Science (Memorial Drive) along the Boston side of the Charles through the Esplanade to Watertown Square. The trail then crosses the river to the Cambridge side on its way back to the Museum of Science. The problem with this bike path is that it's hard to enjoy the scenery when cars are zooming next to you. There are very few places on the trail to escape the noise.

On the South Shore, the **Myles Standish State Forest** has 16 miles of bike trails. To get there, take exit 5 off Route 3 and head west on Long Pond Road. Follow signs to Myles Standish State Forest.

There's also a 7.2-mile bike path along the Cape Cod Canal that runs under the Sagamore and Bourne Bridges. This ride is described in detail under "Road Biking."

For more information on bike paths throughout the region, contact www.railtrails.org. The following trips are three of the better bike loops in New England:

Lincoln/Concord/Carlisle Loop. *Distance:* 26 miles (loop). *Time:* 3 hours to a full day. *Difficulty:* Moderate. *Directions:* From Boston or Cambridge, take Route 2 to Route 126 South. Turn left at Codman Road and left at Lincoln Road. Park on the left-hand side at the Mall at Lincoln Square, in the town of Lincoln.

This ride will satiate all history buffs, whether your specialty is art, architecture, literature, or general American history. Stops on the loop include the sculpture garden at DeCordova Museum, the Gropius House (built by architect Walter Gropius), Thoreau's Walden Pond, the Old Manse (former home of Ralph Waldo Emerson and Nathaniel Hawthorne), and Minute Man National Historical Park, site of the first battle of the Revolutionary War. To top it off, you ride through miles of pastoral backcountry roads in the town of Carlisle.

From the mall parking lot, turn left onto the bike path that hugs Lincoln Road. After another left onto Sandy Pond Road, you'll see the sign for the **DeCordova Museum** on the right-hand side. Set on a hill overlooking Sandy Pond, the grounds of this intimate museum feature large contemporary sculptures.

Once you've had your fill of art, continue on Sandy Pond Road and turn left onto Baker Bridge Road. At 68 Baker Bridge Road stands the **Gropius House.** Walter Gropius was a leading proponent of modern architecture and the founder of the Bauhaus Movement in Germany. He built this house for himself in 1938 after accepting a teaching position at Harvard's Graduate School of Design. Gropius combined traditional elements of New England architecture—brick, fieldstone, and clapboard—with innovative materials rarely seen in houses, such as welded steel, chrome banisters, and glass blocks.

Tour the structure and then head back to Baker Bridge Road, which soon connects with Route 126. Veer right, and on the left side of the road **Walden Pond** soon appears. On July 4, 1845, 28-year-old Henry David Thoreau moved into a spare cabin he had built on the side of Walden Pond. For two years, two months, and two days, the naturalist and philosopher retreated from society and roughed it in the woods. He recounted every experience in his journal, and seven years later published *Walden,* destined to become one of the most widely known books in American history. Today, Walden Pond is among Boston's favorite swimming holes, and its beaches are lined with towels and suntanners in the summertime. Stone posts mark the site of Thoreau's cabin, which was later used as a pig shed before being dismantled for lumber. Lock your bike and wander into Walden Woods, the 2,680-acre area that encompasses the pond (see "Walks and Rambles"). Sixty-five percent of Walden Woods is protected from development, including a parcel bought by the Walden Woods Project, a land trust formed in 1990.

Back on Route 126, cross Route 2 and be wary of traffic. Route 126 turns into Walden Street as you approach the historic hamlet of Concord. Turn right on Main Street and go halfway around the rotary, veering right again onto Monument Street. Your next stop is the **Old Manse,** a three-story house on the left-hand side of the road. Built in 1770 for the Reverend William Emerson, the Old Manse is best known as the place where grandson Ralph Waldo Emerson wrote his book *Nature* and as the home of Nathaniel Hawthorne and his new bride Sophia. The Hawthornes rented the home from 1842 to 1845 for an annual rent of $100. Nathaniel's desk faced a wall on the second floor to help him concentrate on his writing. It worked, for at the young age of 22, he wrote the successful short story *Mosses from an Old Manse*. Sophia, an artist, etched statements with her wedding ring on glass windows around the house. Comments regarding her children and the weather can still be seen on several panes. Outside, Thoreau planted a garden as a wedding gift to the Hawthornes. The grounds are a good place to picnic before walking to **Minute Man National Historical Park** next door.

On the morning of April 19, 1775, a small group of Minutemen met the British Redcoats at this spot. The British had been dispatched from Concord to seize arms and supplies that the provincials had hidden at Barrett Farm on the other side of the Concord River. Before they could cross North Bridge, the Minutemen fired shots. The Redcoats fired back before retreating, and thus the first Revolutionary War battle occurred. On the near side of the Old North Bridge (a reproduction), you can see Daniel Chester French's sculpture *Minuteman*, which he created in 1836 to commemorate the battle. Ralph Waldo Emerson's famous words spoken at the same ceremony are found at the base of the sculpture:

> By the rude bridge that arched the flood
> Their flag to April's breeze unfurled,
> Here once the embattled farmers stood
> And fired the shot heard round the world.

American history soon gives way to century-old rural landscape when you leave Concord and head into Carlisle. Go straight on Monument Street to River Road, lined on both sides by horse farms. Turn left onto Route 225, where you can stop for a scoop of homemade ice cream and pet the goats at Kimball's. Continuing on Route 225, take a

A lighthouse on Cape Ann

sharp left onto Cross Street while you're heading downhill. Here the ride gets tricky as you start to meander on country roads lined with barns, farmland, and recently built mansions.

Nine-tenths of a mile from the junction of Route 225, turn right at a stop sign onto unmarked South Street. A mile later, take a left onto West Street and a quick right onto Pope Road. Your next left will be onto Strawberry Hill Road, 1.2 miles away. Farms have been replaced by large estates that sit on the hillside above. Two miles later, veer left onto Barrett's Mill Road and then right onto Lowell Road. This will bring you back to the rotary in Concord, where you turn right on Main Street and then make a quick left on Walden Street to reach Walden Pond once again. You've now earned a dip in the pond's waters.

After cooling off, proceed on Route 126 to Codman Road. Turn left, veering left once more on Lincoln Road to return to the Mall at

Lincoln Square. You've successfully completed your history course for today.

Cape Ann Loop, North Shore. *Distance:* 26 miles (loop). *Time:* 3 to 6 hours. *Difficulty:* Easy. *Directions:* From Route 128 North, take a right onto Route 133 East and turn right again onto Route 127. The Stage Fort Park in Gloucester is located on the left side of the road. Drive up the hill to find the large parking lot.

Cape Ann is that other Cape—the one we Bostonians like to keep to ourselves. Only 45 minutes to an hour north of Boston via Route 128, Cape Ann juts out into the ocean like a child's hand waving back to the mainland. The Cape Ann region includes not only the island at the tip, but also all the towns that line the peninsula east of Route 1A.

Put blinders on and you can complete the loop around Cape Ann in less than three hours. The rest of us will need twice that amount of time to stop at the many scenic, artistic, and historic offerings. Cruise downhill from Stage Fort Park and turn right where ***The Man at the Wheel*** statue faces the Atlantic Ocean on Pavilion Beach. Created in 1920, this sculpture is a memorial to fishermen who lost their lives at sea. It's a fitting tribute in Gloucester, one of the largest fishing communities on the Atlantic seaboard and the backdrop for Sebastian Junger's book *The Perfect Storm.* If you ride along the harbor in the morning hours, you have an excellent chance of spotting a commercial trawler unloading its day's catch on the docks.

Stay on Route 127 as it curves downhill to Gloucester's **Inner Harbor,** being cautious of the heavy traffic. A granite building sits atop the hill on Harbor Loop. Home to marine artist Fitz Hugh Lane in the mid-19th century, the building was later converted to a prison. Gloucester must have been a relatively safe city in those days, since the house is not much larger than a cottage.

Turn right at the light onto East Main Street, passing the small village of East Gloucester, and bear right again onto **Rocky Neck Avenue.** You are now entering the oldest working art colony in the country. Winslow Homer, Maurice Pendergast, Childe Hassam, and John Frederick Kensett are just a few of the renowned artists who have been lured to Rocky Neck's rugged shores over the past two centuries. It is also the spot where Rudyard Kipling wrote *Captains Courageous* in the company of seamen at the marine railway, which still exists. A quick loop around Rocky Neck's wharf will bring you to a slew of galleries featuring the region's more contemporary talents.

Continue on East Main Street past Niles Beach, turning right between two stone pillars onto Eastern Point Boulevard and its many mansions. You can tour all 45 rooms at one of the houses, **Beauport,** in the summer months. Mansions line both sides of the road all the way to **Eastern Point Lighthouse.** From the lighthouse, join the fishermen on the stone jetty that stretches a half-mile across the mouth of the harbor.

Back on your bike, turn around and veer right onto Farrington Avenue, which soon becomes Atlantic Road. Sweeping vistas of Cape Ann's rocky coastline come into view as you ride along the ocean while the twin lighthouses of Thacher Island hover in the distance. A right turn onto Route 127A (Thacher Road) will bring you to the quaint town of **Rockport.** The strip of stores and restaurants in Bearskin Neck is a great place to find lunch before continuing to the northern part of Cape Ann.

Go straight onto Main Street and veer right onto Beach Street, looking for signs to Pigeon Cove. This will bring you to Route 127 North. Turn right, and in 1 mile you'll see a small State Park sign. The Halibut Point State Park parking lot is less than 100 yards away, to your right. Lock up your bike and cross the street to find the huge rainwater-filled granite quarry (a longer walk to the ocean is described under "Walks and Rambles"). After your stroll, continue on Route 127 to the Annisquam Village Church, where you turn right and bear left twice to get to the small fishing village of **Annisquam.** You may see artists painting the view of the serene harbor as you cross the foot-bridge to return to Route 127.

Bear right, and 3 miles later you'll enter a traffic rotary. Be careful of the oncoming traffic and go halfway around, continuing on Route 127. Turn right on Centennial Avenue for an invigorating downhill run back to Route 127, where you bear right to get back to Stage Fort Park.

Westport Ramble, South Shore. *Distance:* 21 miles (loop). *Time:* 3 hours. *Difficulty:* Easy. *Directions:* From Route 24 South, take Route 195 East for 2 miles to Route 88 South. Turn left at the second traffic light onto Old County Road. A little more than a half-mile later, you'll see Westport Middle School on your left. Park here.

South of Route 195 and the gritty mill towns of Fall River and New Bedford lies countryside so fertile, you'll feel like you're in Vermont. Stretching from Dartmouth, Massachusetts, to Little Compton, Rhode Island, the area is known as the **Heritage Farm Coast.** It has the sunniest, most temperate climate in New England and thus the longest growing season. Vast dairy farms, cornfields, even vineyards border the Westport River as it washes into the Atlantic. Add the dunes of Horseneck Beach and you have the perfect country and coast ride.

Turn left out of the parking lot onto Old County Road to start this loop. A right turn onto Pine Hill Road heads downhill, but the route is relatively flat for most of the ride. Within a mile, you're lost in acres of farmland. Historic Cape Cod shingled houses and barns are bordered by old stone walls. At the 3-mile mark, continue on lightly traveled Old Pine Road to see row upon row of corn edging out onto the horizon.

A mile later, turn right onto Hix Bridge Road and then left a half-mile beyond onto Horseneck Road.

You start to weave through dense forest as you make your way south to the shoreline. Soon the Westport River appears on your right, a strip of dark blue snaking through the emerald green pasture. If you take this ride in the summer, you can purchase produce straight from the farmers—blueberries, sweet corn, tomatoes, whatever the farm happens to be harvesting at the time.

At the 9-mile mark, the ocean starts to appear on your left and the area becomes more developed. You can stop at the **Bayside** for lunch and sample the local wares. Cod wraps, lobster rolls, and fresh salads are a few of the reasonably priced items. Veer right on East Beach Road for expansive views of the ocean. The beach here is rocky and the wind can wreak havoc, so if you want to go for a dip, I'd wait until you reach **Horseneck Beach,** just up the road. Simply turn right onto Route 88 to enter the Horseneck Beach State Reservation. The sweeping beach and dunes can be entered on your left.

After crossing a small bridge, which rewards you with views of the harbor and its numerous fishing boats, turn right at 13.5 miles onto Drift Road. Once again you ride through farmland, yet with views of the Westport River to your right this time. Take Drift Road all the way back to Old County Road, where you turn left to return to the school and your car.

Walks and Rambles

Boston is a walking city, so you'd expect this coastal region to feature some of the most intriguing walks in the book. In addition to the strolls listed, check out **Arnold Arboretum,** just outside of Boston in Jamaica Plain (125 Arborway; 617-524-1718). Every Mother's Day is Lilac Sunday on the 265-acre grounds.

The Freedom Trail, Boston. *Distance:* 3 miles (one way). *Time:* As long as you like. *Difficulty:* Easy. *Directions:* Park on Charles Street, in the large parking garage under Boston Common, to start your walk.

Parents spread out on blankets and mingle with good friends while their children run wild at the nearby playground. Lovers find a secluded spot under the shade of a maple tree, dogs chase Frisbees, a juggler throws balls in the air, and a softball game gets under way on the fringes of the city park. It's a typical summer day. You could be in the main city park of almost any metropolis in America, but inevitably you'll come across one of the numerous plaques that read "Boston Common, America's Oldest Park, Founded in 1634." In Boston, we like to boast about our lengthy history.

We've even created a 3-mile walking route called the Freedom Trail that guides you to the most famous historic sites in the city. You can toss your map in the garbage and simply follow the red line that not only takes you to 16 monumental sites of the past, but also brings you into some of the city's most cherished neighborhoods: Beacon Hill's century-old brick brownstones and village squares, the North End's winding streets and lively Italian community, and Charlestown, site of the Battle of Bunker Hill and the final resting spot of America's most celebrated ship, the USS *Constitution*. The history of America's independence is woven into the fabric of present-day Boston to create a downtown area where the John Hancock Building towers harmoniously over the grave of John Hancock.

From the Common, the Freedom Trail continues at the new **State House.** The gold dome, long one of the city's chief landmarks, was originally fitted with leaky wooden shingles. The trail then goes onward to **Park Street Church,** best known as the spot where on July 4, 1831, the hymn "America" ("My Country 'Tis of Thee") was first sung publicly.

Next door is one of the most popular sites on the walk, the **Granary Burying Ground.** You won't get lost in this absurdly small plot, the final resting spot for Paul Revere, Samuel Adams, John Hancock, Peter Faneuil, the victims of the Boston Massacre—and even a Mother Goose, though historians are not positive if she is *the* Mother Goose. There is no pomp surrounding the Granary, just layer after layer of short stubby headstones that reflect off the windows of a neighboring office building.

From here, you can pass **King's Chapel,** which infuriated every Puritan when it was built in 1687 as the first Anglican parish, and stop at the opposite end of School Street, at every writer's favorite place, the **Old Corner Book Store.** This small brick house, now the Boston Globe Store, rose to prominence in the mid-1800s when it was the offices of Ticknor and Fields, the nation's leading publisher of the day. Ralph Waldo Emerson, Henry David Thoreau, Nathaniel Hawthorne, and Harriet Beecher Stowe were among the authors who gathered here to discuss their newest works.

Three of the most important sites of the American Revolution lie just ahead—the Old South Meeting House, the Old State House, and Faneuil Hall. On December 16, 1773, some seven thousand citizens came to **Old South Meeting House,** spilling out into the streets to protest the Tea Act. When the governor refused for the final time to take his tea back to England, Samuel Adams rose and said, "Gentlemen, this meeting can do nothing more to save the country." Thus the start of the Boston Tea Party.

The first bloodshed of the Revolution took place just outside the **Old State House.** In the Boston Massacre, five colonists were killed when a squad of British officers fired into a taunting, jeering mob.

Constructed in 1742, **Faneuil Hall** was a market where country-folk could sell their produce. Far more important was the meeting hall on the second floor, where colonists like John Hancock first dared to speak publicly against the British. Today the meeting hall still stands, but tacky gift shops have replaced produce stands on the first floor. However, at least one of the businesses downstairs is a unique attraction worth a visit. The **Boston City Store** sells pieces of surplus city property that have outlasted their usefulness. Among the items for sale: street signs from the '50s and '60s ($30), a pair of firefighter boots ($80), streetlights ($325), and a set of seats from the now defunct Boston Garden ($750).

Next to Faneuil Hall is Boston's number one attraction, **Quincy Market.** Hundreds of name-brand shops beckon out-of-towners, many of them just generic versions of chain stores (The Gap, The Body Shop, Crate & Barrel, etc.). Also inside Quincy Market is one long corridor devoted entirely to take-out food. You'll also find one of Boston's best-loved restaurants, **Durgin Park,** which serves hearty Yankee meals like prime rib with Boston baked beans. Diners sit family-style at long tables where surly waitresses are known to throw one or two barbs at you.

The ugliest stretch of the Freedom Trail goes under the highway from Quincy Market to the North End. Instead of turning right with the Freedom Trail, continue straight for one block on Salem Street and then turn right to catch up with the red line back on Hanover Street. This is the authentic **North End** where everything is Italian, from the butcher to the baker to the ravioli maker. Many of the finest restaurants and pastry shops line Hanover Street, including Mike's, which is always crowded with cannoli lovers.

Long before this community was Italian, the North End was Boston's first neighborhood, inhabited since the town's founding in 1630. Standing on a small cobblestone square in the North End is Boston's oldest existing building, the **home of Paul Revere.** Late on the night of April 18, 1775, this middle-aged silversmith set out from here on a journey that would make him one of the most celebrated American patriots. Revere's midnight horseback ride would take him 15 miles to Lexington to warn John Hancock and Samuel Adams of the rapidly moving British troops. It would be close to a year before he dared to set foot in his home again. Remarkably, the two-story structure that Revere bought when it was already 90 years old is still intact. Walk up the spiral wooden staircase to see the dresser and chair Revere used in his bedroom.

Continue on Hanover Street before veering left through the Paul Revere Mall to the **Old North Church.** While Revere was already on his way to Lexington, his friend Robert Newman was instructed to hang lanterns from Old North's steeple windows, "one, if by land, and two, if by sea." This action would alert the people of Charlestown of the British movement just in case Revere never made it to Lexington. Inside Old North, today's congregation still uses the same tall box pews colonists needed to ward off the cold in the harsh years before central heating arrived.

Robert Newman is buried just up the hill from Old North at the North End's highest point, **Copp's Hill Burying Ground.** Inside the graveyard, you'll get your first glimpse of the Charles River and the mast of the USS *Constitution,* which is docked across the water in Charlestown. To reach the hull of Old Ironsides and Bunker Hill, follow the Freedom Trail on the footpath across Charlestown Bridge.

Technically, the **Battle of Bunker Hill** was a British victory since the Redcoats held the bloody summit when it was all over. The Americans were entrenched atop the hill, and to conserve gunpowder were ordered not to fire "'til you see the whites of their eyes." Row after row of Redcoats advanced up the hill, wondering why there was no response. Finally the colonists were ordered to fire. The British were mowed down by the patriots' guns, but soon the Americans did indeed run out of powder. To commemorate this heroic effort, the Bunker Hill Monument, a 221-foot granite obelisk, was dedicated in 1843.

Bostonians like to save the best for last and this is certainly true of the Freedom Trail. Stroll down to the docks of the Charlestown Navy Yard and have a look at the **USS *Constitution*.** Remarkably intact, the sails are pearly white, the hull freshly painted black, and all the sheets look new and tightly coiled. Everything is in shipshape. To celebrate its bicentennial in 1997, Old Ironsides was totally rerigged in order to sail for the first time in more than a century.

The boat's nickname comes from its mighty hull, which was built of live oak. Cannonballs literally bounced off her sides and fell into the sea. Her greatest exploits came during the War of 1812, when she almost single-handedly annihilated the British fleet. Loaded with numerous cannons, the *Constitution* is still an active commissioned ship in the U.S. Navy.

You can now retrace your steps along the Freedom Trail, but more preferable is the one-dollar ferry ride from the Charleston Navy Yard to the Long Wharf, situated close to Faneuil Hall. The 3-mile Freedom Trail can be toured in one day, but then you'll never have the chance to savor the charm of each neighborhood or soak up the wealth of history each stop offers. Paul Revere, Samuel Adams, and John Hancock didn't gain their freedom in a day, so what's the hurry? The route is best taken over the course of two days, preferably on a weekend. This way, the churches are all open, pushcart vendors are selling their fresh produce at Haymarket, the North End could very well be having a *festa,* an Italian festival, and magicians, sword swallowers, mimes, and other performers are out in full force at Quincy Market and Boston Common.

Boston Harbor Islands. *Distance:* Varies. *Time:* At least a day. *Difficulty:* Easy. *Directions:* Ferries depart from Long Wharf, situated next to the New England Aquarium at Central Wharf in downtown Boston.

Quick: Name the group of islands containing the oldest continuously manned lighthouse (Boston Harbor Light) in the country, a vintage Civil War fort, and the place where pirates were hanged in chains as a "spectacle for the warning of others"? Hint: No other area in the United States has so many islands so close to a major city.

These are the Boston Harbor Islands. If you guessed incorrectly, don't despair. You'll be hearing much more about these 31 islands now that they are part of the national park system. The harbor has made a remarkable turnaround since 1988, when Vice President George Bush stood with the murky water behind him and pronounced it the filthiest in the nation. His opinion was exaggerated, a political ploy to harp on the environmental record of his opponent at the time, Massachusetts Governor Michael Dukakis. Yet no one will deny that the Boston Harbor and its islands were misused and ignored for decades, even centuries.

No longer. Under a court-ordered $3.4 billion cleanup program, dumping has ceased and water quality has vastly improved. Porpoises, harbor seals, and striped bass have returned in great numbers, and beaches, staffed by lifeguards, are now open.

The centerpiece of the new national park, **Boston Harbor Islands National Recreation Area,** is **Georges Island,** dominated by the huge, granite Fort Warren. Take the 45-minute ferry ride from Boston's Long Wharf to Georges Island, which rewards you with the best view of the Boston skyline. You'll cruise by a black-and-white-lined channel marker that designates the site of **Nix's Mate,** formerly an island but now just a shoal. In the 1700s, captured pirates were said to have spent their final hours on this 12-acre island.

142

Fort Warren was built in 1833 to defend the United States against a possible invasion. However, it wasn't until the Civil War that the island gained notoriety as a training ground for Union Troops and a prison camp for more than two thousand Confederate soldiers, including the vice president of the Confederacy, Alexander Stephens. To enter this impregnable defense system, you walk across a moat on a drawbridge and slip through an iron gate. Inside, hand-carved spiral staircases crawl up to ramparts and powder magazines, none of which were ever used in battle.

From Georges, you can board a smaller ferry toward **Grape Island.** Here, history is replaced by unbridled nature, an ideal spot for strolling on grassy paths past fields of wild roses, sumac bushes, pines, towering birches, and thickets of blackberries and raspberries. Walk to the top of this glacial drumlin and view the wild landscape. You'll feel like Columbus exploring an undiscovered island. Sailboats tack to and fro in front of Boston's tallest buildings, and although the city is in sight, the hustle and bustle of urbanity seems hundreds of miles away. Overnight camping is available here as well as on neighboring **Lovell Island** (popular for its outer beach) and **Bumpkin Island.**

In summer, the ferry goes to Georges Island and then continues on to Grape, Gallops, Lovell, Peddocks, and Bumpkin Islands. Swimming is allowed only at Lovell. Georges is the only island that has a snack bar, but the ferry serves food and beverages. For ferry schedules, call **Boston Harbor Cruises** at 617-227-4321.

Great Meadows National Wildlife Refuge, near Concord. *Distance:* 1.7 miles (loop). *Time:* 1 hour. *Difficulty:* Easy. *Directions:* From the center of Concord, just west of Boston, follow Route 62 East for 1.8 miles to Monsen Road. Turn left and look for the clearly marked signs to the refuge.

Walking on Grape Island in the Boston Harbor Islands

A chorus of birds is the welcome committee at the Great Meadows National Wildlife Refuge. Bright goldfinches and common yellowthroats whisk from red maple to red maple at the beginning of the Dike Trail. The best is yet to come. As you cross the open-water marsh and uplands, black-crowned night herons dip their beaks into the water like mechanical oil wells. Nearby, great blue herons and families of Canada geese search for food.

Walk straight to the Concord River and then retrace your steps, taking a left and continuing in a clockwise fashion around the swamp. Red-winged blackbirds flash their brilliant streak of color, more vibrant than a Matisse painting, as they fly over cattails and shrubs. A right turn on the Edge Trail will bring you back through the woods to the parking lot. Who would have thought that one of New England's best bird-watching spots is less than a 30-minute drive from Boston?

Walden Pond, near Concord. *Distance:* 1–2 miles. *Time:* Long enough to stroll through the woods. *Difficulty:* Easy. *Directions:* From Concord, just west of Boston, take Route 126 South through the intersection with Route 2. The parking area is on your right.

"I went to the woods because I wished to live deliberately, to front only the essential facts of life, and see if I could not learn what it had to teach, and not, when I came to die, discover that I had not lived," wrote Henry David Thoreau in his best-known work, *Walden.* Thoreau ventured to the woods with ax in tow in March 1845 to build his hut. Never would this modest writer imagine what an impact his philosophical musings would have on the world more than 150 years after he cut down his first tall pine.

For two years, two months, and two days, Thoreau lived in the woods, a mile from any neighbor, in his rustic abode built near the shores of Walden Pond. While the hut no longer exists, the woods make for a wonderful stroll, especially in the early morning hours. A shaded path leads you out to the spot where Thoreau found solitude.

"I never found the companion that was so companionable as solitude," Thoreau wrote in *Walden,* perhaps as a backlash to the hordes of curious visitors who arrived unexpectedly at his house. Most of these uninvited drop-ins were schoolchildren, family members, friends, and other philosophers from Concord and Lincoln.

Almost daily, Thoreau walked to Concord to exchange beans for rice and collect news of his family. The townspeople would frequently ask him if he was lonely. To this he replied, "I am no more lonely than a single mullein or dandelion in a pasture, or a bean leaf, or sorrel, or a horse-fly, or a bumble-bee. I am no more lonely than the Mill Brook, or a weathercock, or the north star, or the south wind, or an April shower, or a January thaw, or the first spider in a new home."

World's End, near Hingham. *Distance:* 4 miles (loop). *Time:* 2 hours. *Difficulty:* Easy. *Directions:* South of Boston, take exit 14 off Route 3 and follow Route 228 North for 6.7 miles. Go left on Route 3A for 0.9 mile to Summer Street, then turn right for another 0.3 mile. Cross Rockland Street to Martin's Lane and go 0.7 mile to the end.

World's End is a drumlin, a gentle hill formed of clay, gravel, and sand left when an ancient glacier retreated. It juts out of Hingham Harbor, looking in shape like a rooster crowing at daybreak. In 1890, landscape architect Frederick Law Olmsted was hired to transform World's End into a community of 150 homes. Thankfully this never came to fruition. The 251-acre hill was farmed and owned by one family until The Trustees of Reservations, a nonprofit organization that maintains over 75 preserves in the state, purchased the property with the help of the public in 1967.

To start your walk (jogging is also popular here), head to the end of the parking lot and proceed past the chain onto a wide path bordered by white pines, hickories, oaks, and bracken ferns. Continue along the trail in a counterclockwise fashion, starting with the rooster's tail first. A right turn through a row of sugar maples will bring you to the rocky outcroppings that form the shoreline of Weir River. The path narrows as it hugs the rocky shores, clambering over boulders, before reaching the broad main trail again. Turn right and head across the constructed sand spit to World's End proper.

Another right turn will lead you around the perimeter of this drumlin. Bumpkin Island obstructs the views of Boston Harbor and the city's skyline. However, once you turn right, cross the sand bar again, and walk to the top of Planter's Hill, you can see across Hingham Bay to Boston and the islands of its harbor. Head straight down the hill to return to the parking lot.

Halibut Point State Park, North Shore. *Distance:* 1.5 miles. *Time:* 1 hour. *Difficulty:* Easy. *Directions:* From downtown Rockport, take Route 127 North past Pigeon Cove to a small green sign that says State Park. This is Gott Avenue. Turn right and you'll see the much larger Halibut Point State Park sign and a parking lot.

At Halibut Point State Park and Reservation, you have the unique opportunity to visit a huge quarry once used by the Rockport Granite Company and a boulder train that slopes down to the ocean. The park did not get its name from the fish, but from sailors who tacked around Cape Ann at this point and yelled "Haul about!"

Cross Gott Avenue and continue on the wood chip–lined path to the small roundabout. Just before you turn right, you'll notice a large oval slab of granite that was used as a mooring for a fishing boat's anchorage. The mooring is one of the many chunks of rock ripped out of the earth from the quarry. The quarry hole is now filled with 60-plus years of blackened rainwater, providing a mirrorlike reflection of the clouds and granite walls.

Several hundred yards past the quarry, a narrow trail off to the right leads through the brush. Turn right through the scrub oak, shadbush, and greenbrier, and you'll soon come to a wide gravel path. At the next juncture, turn left to continue through the brush to the large rock pile or go straight on the boulders that line the shore. Veer left onto the large gravel path that leads to an overlook atop the rock pile. Plum Island and the shores of New Hampshire can be seen to your left on a clear day.

Returning to the main trail, veer right and turn right again at the two black cherry trees to reach the Bayview Trail. This path is a quick loop along the ocean, where black cormorants and other marine birds sit atop rocky perches. A left turn at park headquarters will give you one last glance at the quarry before you retrace your steps on the trail back to Gott Avenue and the parking area.

TWO, IF BY SEA

Canoeing

A slew of rivers and ponds in the Greater Boston area attract canoeists. On the South Shore, the North River meanders more than 20 miles from the sparsely populated headwaters at Hanson and Hanover to the ocean just south of Scituate. It's not uncommon to find herons, warblers, terns, and red-winged blackbirds flying over the waters. Most people paddle west of the Union Street Bridge in Norwell, avoiding the deadly riptide where the North and South Rivers meet. **King's Landing Marina** (781-659-7273) off Route 123 in Norwell rents canoes for the North River.

In Boston and the northern suburbs, canoeing is popular on the 80-mile-long Charles River (see "Sculling"). Canoes can be rented from the **Charles River Canoe and Kayak Center** (617-965-5110) in Newton and Boston.

Northwest of Boston, the Concord River has changed little since Thoreau ventured here and wrote *A Week on the Concord and Merrimack Rivers*. Rent a canoe from the **South Bridge Boat House** (496-502 Main Street, Concord; 978-369-9438) and paddle under Old North Bridge and through Minute Man National Historical Park, following the migrating birds to Great Meadows National Wildlife Refuge. The round-trip on this river lined with silver maples, birches, and oaks takes about four hours.

The following are several canoeing jaunts worth a closer look.

Ipswich River, Topsfield; North Shore. *Distance:* 7 miles (one way). *Time:* 4 hours. *Difficulty:* Easy. *Directions:* From the Boston area, take Route 1 North past the fairgrounds at Topsfield and turn right at the second light onto Ipswich Road. Continue 3 miles to Foote Brothers Canoe Rentals.

The Ipswich River north of Boston, snaking through the largest wildlife sanctuary administered by the Massachusetts Audubon Society, is a bird lover's delight. The folks at Foote Brothers Canoe Rentals will drive you to the Salem Road put-in to begin the jaunt back to the rental outpost.

The Ipswich is one of those narrow, serpentine rivers that was designed for canoeists. The glasslike waters of the river are interrupted only by the occasional tree limb jutting up into the air. Paddle under three bridges, veering left at the last bridge, and keep your eyes open for birdies. Snowy egrets usually stand tall in the marsh, eastern kingbirds nest on overhanging branches, and the iridescent blue-green head

Paddling the Ipswich River in Topsfield

of the common grackle can be spotted as the bird eagerly searches for food on the banks of the river. Also be on the lookout for Mama Mallard and her row of fuzzy chickadees, large turtles resting on rotted-out logs, and the call of the bullfrog, sounding like a broken guitar string.

Perkins Island is a fine spot to stop for lunch and reenergize for the remainder of the trip. The river continues to curve through fields of unadulterated forest, slowly starting to widen as it approaches Foote Brothers. The Salem Run costs $30 per canoe. You can also rent canoes at the outpost and paddle upstream for $20 a canoe or take the 9.75-mile Thunder Bridge Run for $35. Call **Foote Brothers** at 978-356-9771.

Essex River Basin, Essex; North Shore. See the writeup under "Sea Kayaking" on page 158.

Slocum River, Dartmouth; South Shore. *Distance:* 8 miles (round-trip).

Time: 3 to 5 hours. *Difficulty:* Easy. *Directions:* South of Boston, take Route 24 South and then take I-195 East to exit 12. From the exit go south, crossing Route 6 and continuing straight, following signs to Demarest Lloyd State Park. Park here.

The South Shore's answer to the Essex River is the tidal Slocum River, offering a well-protected jaunt near Buzzards Bay. Paddle upstream past the young families that congregate on the Demarest Lloyd beach, and around a bend to the left is **Giles Creek.** This is a good place to spot herons and egrets lounging in the salt marsh. The river widens as you pass Pelegs Island, but then narrows just as quickly. Four miles from the put-in, you will reach the small town of **Russells Mills.** If you're hungry, you can visit the general store just down Horseneck Road to the right. Otherwise, have a leisurely paddle back.

Massasoit State Park, Taunton; southeastern Massachusetts. *Distance:* 2–3 miles. *Time:* As long as you're content. *Difficulty:* Easy. *Directions:* Take I-495 to exit 5 and head south on Route 18. Less than a mile later, turn right onto Middleboro Avenue, following signs to Massasoit State Park. After 2.4 miles, you'll see the boat launch for **Lake Rico** (just past the park entrance). Park at the small lot on your left.

Perhaps the finest lake paddling in eastern Massachusetts is at Lake Rico and a series of ponds in little-known Massasoit State Park. The lake offers several miles of shoreline canoeing without the hum of motors. All these bodies of water are off-limits to motorboats. Head south from the launch area past thickets of pine and eventually you'll reach the marsh of **Kings Pond,** a favorite spot for great blue and green herons. Back in the deep water, you can fish for pickerel and perch.

Canoeing through Massasoit State Park in Taunton

Fishing

Considering Gloucester is the oldest fishing port in America, how can you go wrong with saltwater fishing in this region? Surf-cast for blues between late July and early October and stripers starting in late May. Then there are the cod looking for herring in early May before the stripers come in town. For bait, use poppers during the day and sand eels at night for the blues; sand eels during the day and live eels at night for stripers. Stripers also love raw clams.

In Boston, some of the best action is at the Charles River Locks and Charlestown Dam and the Castle Island Pier. On the North Shore, schools of fishermen congregate on the beaches of Plum Island at the mouth of the Merrimack and Parker Rivers.

On the South Shore, anglers head to Humarock Beach to fish at the mouths of both the North and South Rivers. Other popular South Shore locales include the end of Fourth Cliff in Scituate and Third Cliff Beach on the seawall, and the rocks overlooking Plymouth Harbor. Just find the seagulls swarming and diving into the water and you'll find the blues. The gulls are looking for leftover pieces of fish flesh, the result of a bluefish feeding frenzy.

Scup, tautog, fluke, sea bass, and other bottom fish are found when you venture offshore. There's also the chance you'll catch cod, pollock, haddock, mackerel, flounder, and tuna. For boats out of Boston, try **Firefly Outfitter** (617-423-3474). On the North Shore, contact the **Yankee Fishing Fleet,** Gloucester (978-283-0313 or 1-800-942-5464; www.yankee-fleet.com) or **Captain Bill's** in Gloucester (978-283-6995; www.captainbillswhalewatch.com). Deep-sea fishing trips on the South Shore can be arranged through **Andy Lynn Boats,** Plymouth (508-746-7776); **Captain John Boats,** Plymouth (508-746-2643; www.captjohn.com); and **Captain Tim Brady & Sons,** Plymouth (508-746-4809).

For freshwater fishing, there's no need to travel too far from Boston. Fishing at **Jamaica Pond** is almost entirely by boat, which may be rented at the boathouse. Jamaica Pond is in Jamaica Plain: take the Riverway south from Route 9. The pond will be on your right. Take the kids for their first fishing outing or enter one of the many fishing events. The well-stocked pond is home to many browns, rainbows, and brookies. Spring-fed Walden Pond at Concord also has its heavy supply of trout. Both are good spots for casual fishing in the dense city.

North of Boston, the Merrimack River is a worthy spot to catch shad and stripers on the fly. The hot spot is just below Lawrence Dam. Take I-495 to Route 28 and you'll see the parking area and picnic spot.

On the South Shore, the 100-foot-deep Long Pond in Plymouth has large browns, well-stocked rainbows, brookies, and perch. The best times to fish here are spring and fall. In the summer the place gets too busy.

Sailing

Learning to sail in Boston Harbor is like learning to drive on L.A.'s highways. The traffic is often unrelenting. Tugboats guide large oil tankers into the wharves; ferries make quick jaunts to the Boston Harbor Islands; and jets flying into Boston's Logan Airport are so close that you can often see the rivets on an airplane's underside. Yet that doesn't deter the hundreds of sailors who relish the opportunity on a clear summer day to find their own cruising ground in the water. The rewards are great. The wind is always at a good 15- to 20-knot clip. Boston's shimmering skyline is best seen from the water. And once you venture outside the port, traffic diminishes and you could very well find yourself picnicking on a deserted island. Most important, if you learn to sail here amid all this chaos, you'll pick up the necessary skills to sail almost anywhere in the world.

Boston Sailing Center (617-227-4198; www.bostonsailingcenter.com) at Lewis Wharf and **Boston Harbor Sailing Club** (617-720-0049; www.by-the-sea.com/bhsclub/) at Rowes Wharf have been teaching novices the sport for more than 20 years. They offer learn-to-sail, advanced, and cruising courses that will have students ready to bareboat charter by the end of the summer. Instruction is aboard Solings, J-24s, and J-30s and is taught by some of the saltiest dogs on the Atlantic Seaboard. If you incorrectly tie a bowline or half-hitch, you'll hear about it immediately from the instructors. A far worse scolding is in store if you motor too fast into the dock, do an uncontrolled jibe, or hastily fold your sails. But during the five-week learn-to-sail course, instructors have the keen ability to turn lumpy landlubbers into proficient sailors.

Each week, you'll head farther out into the Boston Harbor Islands. These small specks of land, 31 islands in all, are now part of the

Sailing off Marion

National Park System. Several of the islands, like remote Calf Island, have sandy beaches and coves, ideal for anchorages. (For more information on the Boston Harbor Islands, see "Walks and Rambles").

Both schools also offer a cruising course, where you glide by the Harbor Islands and head north along the Atlantic coast to Cape Ann. Under dark skies, you'll learn how to navigate at night by listening to the clangs of buoys and watching for signals from distant lighthouses. In the daytime, instructors will discuss the mechanical and electrical systems of the boat as you sail past the deserted beaches of Plum Island into Rockport's picturesque harbor.

North and south of Boston are legendary cruising grounds, where long inlets hide yachting hamlets like Marblehead, Rockport, and Cohasset. On the North Shore, Bert Williams, founder of the **Coastal Sailing School** (781-639-0553; www.coastalsailingschool.com), has taught thousands how to sail in the Atlantic. He uses a 30-foot sloop for his courses in Marblehead. On the southeastern shores, Marion and Padanarum are gateways to Buzzards Bay. Protected by the Elizabeth Islands, which also make for good anchorages, these small towns have been a haven for Massachusetts yachters over the years.

Scuba Diving

Why pay $15 for a lobster at a restaurant when you can find your own crustacean on the floor of the ocean? Whether you dive from a boat or simply walk in from the beach, the Atlantic offers an unlimited number of diving opportunities, from wreck diving to hanging with harbor seals. In Boston, contact **East Coast Divers** (617-277-2216; www.ecdivers.com), with locations in Brookline and Framingham.

On Cape Ann, there are a number of shipwrecks, wall dives, and rocky reefs just off the shore. Charters and instruction are provided by **Cape Ann Divers** in Gloucester (978-281-8082; www.capeann divers.com).

Divers on the South Shore head to Brant Rock Public Beach in Marshfield and the wrecks off Scituate. **North Atlantic Scuba** in Marshfield (781-834-4087) rents all the necessary equipment. Charters are offered by **Andy Lynn** in Plymouth (508-746-7776).

Sculling

Boston's Charles River is home to the Harvard crew team and hundreds of other rowers who yearn to be on the Harvard crew team. On a warm day in summer, there are probably more sculls on the Charles than on the Thames in Oxford, especially between the Museum of Science and the B.U. Bridge. From the B.U. Bridge, the river snakes through Allston and Brighton to Watertown. The **Charles River Canoe and Kayak Center** rents sculls and provides lessons. They have locations in Newton (617-965-5110) and in Boston (617-462-2513).

Learning to scull, however, is not easy. Both oars have to be together at all times or the boat quickly tips to the left or right. Many beginners spend the better part of the first day in the water as they try to balance the boat. It's best to think of the oars as a bike chain and to move in that oval-like fashion. Legs are thrust up against a board for pushing off and scooting your behind back as you propel the oars forward. Many scullers have immense quad muscles, proving that legs are more important than arms in the stroke.

Once you have the stroke down, you next have to contend with moving backward. Novices often get tangled up, because it's one of the few sports where you have to turn your head around to see where you are. But once you get in a flow, all is forgotten as you quickly skim across the Charles. Folks who use the rowing machine at the local gym know what a great workout sculling is for the whole body. It's far superior when you're cruising along a river in the heart of Boston.

Sea Kayaking

If you're feeling intrepid, sea kayak around the Boston Harbor Islands—but paddle quickly when you see the wake of a large tugboat sucking you in. Indeed, the area around Hull is becoming increasingly popular with sea kayakers.

Even more daring, kayak with whales. **Adventure Learning** in Merrimac (978-346-9728; www.adventure-learning.com), on the North Shore, will transport you and five other kayakers out to sea to Stellwagen Bank or Jeffrey's Ledge on the *Rainbow Chaser,* a large motorboat. Once at the bank, you have the rare and exhilarating opportunity to glide eye-to-eye with humpback and minke whales. Since there is always the possibility of rough weather, kayakers should be experienced. The cost of the one-day outing is $130. Adventure Learning also leads guided day trips to Plum Island, Thacher Island, Cape

Ann, and Marblehead Harbor and offers sea kayaking clinics.

For one of the premier kayaking day trips along the Eastern Seaboard, try the following Cape Ann treasure.

Essex River Basin, Essex; North Shore. *Distance:* 5–6 miles (round-trip). *Time:* 3 to 6 hours. *Difficulty:* Moderate. *Directions:* From Route 128 North, take exit 15 (School Street) and veer left, traveling for 3 miles into the town of Essex. Park behind Woodman's seafood stand. Across the street is a small boat launch. Be wary of changing tides: there's a differential of 8 to 10 feet, so plan accordingly.

Less than an hour's drive north of Boston, Essex Marsh is several thousand acres of tidal creek accessible via the Essex and Castle Neck Rivers. In the middle of the Marsh sits **Hog Island,** a perfect place to picnic or stroll. At the put-in, paddle north (preferably with the tide going out). This area is rich with bird life. The river widens as you make your way around Hog Island.

The best place to stop is at the northern tip of Hog Island, where it connects to Long Island. From here, a trail maintained by The Trustees of Reservations leads through spruce forest planted by plumbing magnate Richard Crane. Crane purchased the entire island and a great deal of the surrounding landscape in the early 1900s. After your little walk, kayak back to the put-in (hopefully with the tide going in).

Once you tire from a day of breathing in the salty mist of the sea, reenergize back at Woodman's. Even in the off-season, it's not unusual to find a line out the door at this Essex seafood shack. People queue up to order lobsters of every size imaginable, buckets of tender Ipswich clams, fried shrimp, corn on the cob, and mounds of onion rings. The signature dish is the fried clam platter. Conventional wisdom has it that the fried clam was invented at Woodman's on July 3, 1916. Lawrence Dexter "Chubby" Woodman was frying potato chips for the

Fourth of July celebration when someone suggested that he drop a few steamers into the hot fat. The rest is mouth-watering history. To this day, Woodman's is still run by seven members of the Woodman clan. You can sit at one of the picnic tables inside the restaurant or, better yet, head outside and have dinner on the edge of the Essex River Basin. The pencil-thin legs of blue herons can often be seen standing deep in the beds of these estuarine mudflats as the birds search for their own bucket of clams.

Essex River Basin Adventures in Essex (978-768-3722; www. erba.com) offers three- to five-hour tours from the estuaries of the Essex River to Plum Island, Thacher Island, Hog Island, or over to Crane Beach.

Surfing

On the North Shore, surfers hone their skills at Long Beach in Rockport, Good Harbor Beach in Gloucester, and Plum Island in Newburyport. On the South Shore, check out Nantasket Beach in Hull. This is not the Pipeline, so a wet suit is advisable. The **Nor'Easter Surf Shop** on the South Shore in Scituate (781-544-9283) offers private lessons on nearby Egypt Beach. They also sponsor free afternoon surf camps for novices. Boards provided.

Whale Watching

You don't have to go all the way to Provincetown to catch a whale-watching cruise to Stellwagen Bank, the 18-mile-long underwater mesa that's 7 miles north of Provincetown, 25 miles east of Boston, and 12 miles southeast of Gloucester. The many fish on the bank attract whales from April to November, including humpbacks, finbacks, and minkes. For information on whale cruises, you can contact the **New England Aquarium** in Boston (617-973-5281; www.neaq.org/visit/whalewatch.

html). **Yankee Whale Watching** (1-800-942-5464; www.yankee-fleet. com) runs four- to five-hour trips from Gloucester. From the South Shore, at Plymouth, you can take a four-hour cruise with **Captain John Boats** (Town Wharf; 1-800-242-2469; www.whalewatchingplymouth. com).

Wind Surfing

On the North Shore, strong winds are commonly found off the shores of Plum and Nahant Islands. On the South Shore, wind surfers head to Duxbury Bay, near Marshfield. The bay is good for shortboarding since it's protected by Duxbury Beach.

A DAY AT THE BEACH

On hot summer days, Bostonians don't need to travel far to find a long stretch of sand. Not surprisingly, the waters of the Atlantic are just as frigid here as they are in Cape Cod.

Let's start from the north, with the white sands of 4.5-mile-long **Crane Beach,** and work our way south. Located on the North Shore, east of Ipswich, Crane's smooth shallow surf and dunes are popular with families. Watch out for those nasty greenhead flies that invade the beach in mid-July.

Plum Island Beach and **Salisbury Beach** are two more large strips of sand that attract families. Federally protected piping plovers nest on Plum Island, closing the beach for most of the summer. Call the Parker River National Wildlife Refuge (978-465-5753) for current information regarding Plum Island.

Rockport and Gloucester have a number of small beaches, but you'll need to arrive early if you want to find a parking spot and a place on the sand. They include **Back, Front, and Long Beaches** in Rockport and **Wingaersheek Beach** in Gloucester. Wingaersheek is a favorite for Boston families who make the 45-minute drive north to swim in the shallow waters. Kids love the large rock formations on the far side of the beach and, at low tide, it feels like you can walk all the way to Annisquam Village. Singles head to **Long Beach** and **Good Harbor Beach** in Gloucester.

Heading farther south, Manchester's **Singing Beach** is tucked away in a cove and backed by cliffs and mansions that reside high on the hills. It's a quiet place for couples, since many families don't want to schlep their belongings from the parking area in town on a 10-minute walk to the beach. Marblehead's **Devereux Beach** has a playground that's fun for children. If you have a boat, head to the beach on **Great Misery Island**, about a half-mile out to sea from Manchester.

On the South Shore, families who like a bit of action head to **Nantasket Beach** in Hull. Arcades, rides, and food stands crowd the busy but clean beach. Near Marshfield, 5-mile-long **Duxbury Beach** is another favorite for families. Then there are Plymouth's long narrow beaches, like **White Horse Beach,** which has great views onto Cape Cod Bay but very little parking. More secluded spots for couples include **Onset Beach** in Wareham and **Rexhame and Humarock Beaches** in Marshfield.

On the southwestern shores, south of New Bedford, a family favorite is **Demarest Lloyd State Park.** The 220-acre park juts out into Slocum River, protected by the winds of Buzzards Bay. With little surf, at low tide children can practically walk across the shallow water to the other side of the river. Singles head to the surf at **Horseneck Beach** in Westport. Easily accessed from I-195 by Route 88 South, Horseneck's dunes and waves attract the South Shore crowds on those sweltering days of summer.

CAMPGROUNDS

Salisbury Beach State Reservation, Salisbury; North Shore (978-462-4481). From Salisbury, head 2 miles east on Route 1A. The facility offers 483 sites (159 without hook-ups), handicapped-accessible rest rooms, hot showers, flush toilets, and grills. Part of a 520-acre property, all sites are on or near the shore. This boat-friendly campground is a good spot for sportfishing.

Harold Parker State Forest, North Andover; North Shore (978-686-3391). From the junction of I-495 and Route 114, head 9 miles south on Route 114. You'll find 125 sites, flush toilets, showers, ice, tables, and fireplaces. The sites here are ideal for mountain bikers and hikers, with numerous trails crisscrossing the 3,500-acre state forest.

Cape Ann Campsite, West Gloucester; North Shore (978-283-8683). From Boston, take Route 128 North to exit 13 and turn right on Concord Street. Another right on Atlantic Street leads to the campground. There are 250 sites (42 with full hook-ups), flush toilets, showers, a snack bar, and ice. This kid-friendly campsite is less than a mile from Wingaersheek Beach. The sites are on 100 acres of woodlands on the shores of saltwater inlets.

Winter Island Park, Salem; North Shore (978-745-9430). From the junction of Derby Street and Fort Avenue in Salem, head northeast on Winter Island Road. The park provides 41 sites (33 without hook-ups), handicapped-accessible rest rooms, a bathhouse, hot showers, a snack bar, ice, grills, and firewood. The park is conveniently located in the historic town of Salem near the ocean, so you can surf-cast for stripers at Fort Pickering, sea kayak in Salem Harbor, or lounge on the Marblehead beaches.

The Boston Harbor Islands

Boston Harbor Islands State Park (617-727-7676 for permits to Lovell and Peddocks Islands; 877-422-6762 for Bumpkin and Grape Islands). The ferry to the islands leaves from downtown Boston at Long Wharf, Hewett's Cove in Hingham, 349 Lincoln Street (Route 3A), and (weekends only) from Blarney Street Pier in Salem. The park offers 41 sites, toilets, handicapped-accessible rest rooms; no water is provided, and open fires are not permitted. These campgrounds are spread over four islands situated in Boston Harbor: Bumpkin, Grape, Lovell, and Peddocks. Each has a minimum of 10 to 12 camps. Lovell has supervised swimming.

Wompatuck State Park, south of Hingham; South Shore (781-749-7160). Take Route 3 south of Boston to exit 14. Drive north on Route 228 and look for signs to the park. At the park are 400 sites (140 with electrical hook-ups), showers, flush toilets, picnic tables, piped water, and fireplaces. This is a favorite mountain biking park. You're also close to Nantasket Beach in Hull and the walk at World's End.

Myles Standish State Forest, South Carver; South Shore (508-866-2526). From Federal Furnace Road in South Carver, head 3 miles west on Cranberry Road. There are 475 sites, handicapped-accessible rest rooms, hot showers, ice, and grills. Providing the largest camping facility in any Massachusetts state forest or park, this 14,000-acre state forest is only a few miles from the shores of Plymouth. Sixteen miles of trails in the park are reserved for bikers, and the ponds are stocked with bass, perch, and pickerel.

Sandy Pond Campground, Plymouth; South Shore (508-759-9336). From Boston, take Route 3 South to exit 3. Turn right off the ramp and make a quick left onto Long Pond Road. Drive 1.7 miles and turn right onto Halfway Pond Road. After 0.7 mile, turn left on Bourne Road and travel 5.5 miles. The campground is on your right. It provides 129 sites (most with hook-ups), hot showers, flush toilets, a store, firewood, ice, and canoe rentals. With 2,000 feet of shoreline on Sandy Pond, this is a great find for swimming and fishing. Some sites are shaded by towering pines.

Horseneck Beach State Reservation, Westport; South Shore (508-636-8816). From Route 24 South, take Route 195 East for 2 miles to Route 88 South. Follow the road to the end. There are 100 sites (none with hook-ups), hot showers, piped water, grills, and a boat ramp. Smack dab on Horseneck Beach, these sites are popular with beach lovers and with boaters who want to explore Buzzards Bay.

CHAPTER FIVE
New Hampshire and Southern Maine

▶ New Hampshire is known for those granite-carved notches called the White Mountains, but the state also borders the Atlantic Ocean for an 18-mile stretch from Massachusetts to Maine. Flat, wide beaches rim the coast all the way north to Cape Elizabeth, just below Portland. That's when the rugged Maine rock takes over and the shoreline changes dramatically with its denouement, the mountains of Acadia National Park.

Thousands of sun worshipers flock to the New Hampshire and southern Maine coasts during the weekends in summer, but that's nothing new. Hampton, in New Hampshire, and Ogunquit and Old Orchard Beach, in Maine, have been honky-tonk beach towns since the turn of the 20th century. The pier at Old Orchard Beach was originally built in 1898, with pavilions housing a casino, restaurants, and animals. Today Route 1 is a busy strip, with more than enough lobster joints, miniature golf courses, and other tourist attractions. You can expect a constant buzz of traffic from June to September.

This means slim pickin's for the outdoor recreation enthusiast, except for beachcombers. However, sea kayakers and anglers can always venture offshore to get away from the crowds. And walkers do have several choices, including Odiorne Point State Park in New Hampshire and the same walk Winslow Homer took every morning at Prouts Neck in Maine. Bikers should look elsewhere in the book for the best rides. Not only does Route 1 hem riders in, but I-95 is very close to the coast here, and the traffic coming off this highway is overwhelming.

THE TERRAIN

Long stretches of sand and silt that rivers once brought down from the hills spread out at the edge of the sea. Rarely does a ridge jut out above the ocean on this broad, flat section of the coast. Just south of Portland, the rocky shores of Maine start to appear.

GETTING HERE

This chapter covers the coast of New Hampshire and southern Maine, including Portland. Interstate 95 and Route 1 cruise from Boston along the New Hampshire shore north into Maine.

The Activities

ONE, IF BY LAND

Ballooning

Hot-air balloon rides are offered by a Portland outfitter with an original name, **Balloon Rides** (17 Freeman Street; 1-800-952-2076).

Birding

Route 1A in New Hampshire from Seabrook to Portsmouth is home to many tidal estuaries and saltwater marshes and, thus, migratory shorebirds. **Seabrook Harbor** is a good locale for year-round birding. In July and August, roseate, Forster's, and common terns can be seen. In September, look for plovers, killdeer, whimbrels, ruddy turnstones, sanderlings, and several kinds of sandpipers. Migrating waterfowl include common loons, common goldeneyes, buffleheads, and common and red-breasted mergansers.

The only spit of undeveloped coastline in New Hampshire, **Odiorne Point State Park** in Portsmouth, has 300 acres of protected coastline. It's a good place to find ring-billed and black-backed gulls feeding along the shore (see "Walks and Rambles"). Watch for double-crested cormorants on the rocks, drying their wings. Interpretive panels are located throughout the park, which also has a small visitor center.

The 5,280-acre Great Bay Estuary is a complex embankment on the New Hampshire/Maine border composed of the Piscataqua River, Little Bay, and Great Bay. Ocean tides and river runoff mix 15 miles inland from the Atlantic Ocean in Durham, making Great Bay one of the most recessed estuaries in the nation. A total of 281 species of birds utilize the estuarine salt marshes, waters, and uplands of **Great Bay National Wildlife Refuge**. Among the more common are ospreys, American black ducks, doublecrested cormorants, and great blue herons. The refuge is also an excellent place to see and hear wild turkeys throughout the year.

Six miles offshore, visitors to the **Isles of Shoals** can spot seabirds such as Wilson's storm-petrels, dovekies, thick-billed murres, and razorbills. During fall and spring migration, you are likely to see a variety of warblers such as Wilson's, hooded, orange-crowned, mourning, and Cape May. You can arrange boat trips to the islands with the **Isles of Shoals Steamship Company** (Market Street, Portsmouth; 603-431-5500 or 1-800-441-4620 from outside New Hampshire, 1-800-894-5509 from inside the state).

Heading north into Maine, the **Wells Natural Estuarine Reserve** at Laudholm Farm (207-646-1555) consists of 1,600 acres of prime bird-watching habitat. Seven miles of trails wander through woods, wet-lands, and two barrier beaches. Nearby, the **Rachel Carson National Wildlife Refuge** has a 1-mile nature trail through a white pine forest and salt marsh area. It's a great place to spot migrating shorebirds.

The **Scarborough Marsh Nature Center**, 10 miles south of Port-land (207-883-5100), is home to the largest salt marsh in Maine. Run by the Maine Audubon Society, the center offers canoe rentals, guid-ed canoe trips, and walking tours on a 3,000-acre tract of land. The headquarters of the **Maine Audubon Society** are located at the **Gis-land Farm Sanctuary** at Falmouth Foreside (207-781-2330), where 60 acres of trails snake through the rolling fields and salt marsh.

Golf

The oceanside **Portsmouth Country Club** in Greenland (603-436-9719) added a new clubhouse in 1999. Opened in 1957, this Robert Trent Jones gem has fast greens, but the fairways can be rough when windy. In southern Maine, the **Cape Arundel Golf Club** on Old River Road in Kennebunkport (207-967-3494) is the course former President George Herbert Walker Bush plays when he's in town—a scenic layout where play is often delayed by fog. The front nine at the **Biddeford-Saco Country Club** (101 Old Orchard Road, Saco; 207-282-5883) was designed by Donald Ross and is a good course for average golfers. **Sable Oaks Golf Club** (505 Country Club Drive, South Portland; 207-775-6257) has long, well-groomed fairways in great condition.

Hiking

Two small mountains close to the coast are easy 350-foot climbs, ideal for young children who want to bag their first peak.

Blue Job Mountain, New Hampshire. *Distance:* 1 mile (round-trip). *Time:* 1 hour. *Difficulty:* Easy. *Directions:* From Rochester, take Route 202A West and continue on Crown Point Road as Route 202A bears left to Center Strafford. Drive for half a mile to Strafford Corner and continue another 5 miles when you start to see Blue Job Mountain, topped by the tower, on your right. Across from a farmhouse on the left, park before a locked gate leading into a blueberry field. There are no trail signs, but you can follow the service lines into Blue Job's forest.

If you feel like climbing a mountain, but don't want to work too hard, head to Blue Job. The drive to the starting point leaves you at an elevation of 1,000 feet, so it's a mere 356 feet of elevation gain to hike before reaching Blue Job's summit and fire tower. Enter an oak forest and take a right, climbing gradually to the warden's cabin and fire tower. Why not climb the tower? On a clear day, the views are outstanding. You'll be able to clearly see Mount Washington to the north and the Atlantic Ocean to the east.

Mount Agamenticus, Maine. *Distance:* 1 mile (round-trip). *Time:* 1 hour. *Difficulty:* Easy. *Directions:* From I-95, take the York exit and get to the western side of the highway. Turn right (north) on Chase's Pond Road and continue 3 miles to the junction with Mountain Road in Agamenticus Village. Veer left onto Agamenticus Road and take it 2.7 miles until the paved road ends. Park your car at the foot of Summit Road.

This short path starts on an old road through firs and tall pines. When you reach a junction, keep left as the trail gently rises. Head right under the power lines up a series of granite ledges. The trail climbs steadily, reaching Summit Road near the top. Follow the road to the summit, site of a former downhill ski operation, and continue up the fire tower. On clear days, you can see Mount Washington and other peaks in the Presidential Range. You can certainly view the southern Maine coast and the towns of Kittery, Maine, and Portsmouth, New Hampshire.

Horseback Riding

On Maine's South Coast just outside of Wells, the **Mount Agamenticus Riding Stables** offers 1- to 3-hour guided rides (207-361-2840).

Mountain Biking

Rockingham Recreational Trail, Maine. *Distance:* 25 miles (one way). *Time:* 5 to 6 hours. *Difficulty:* Easy. *Directions to the western terminus:* The western end of this trail is close to Manchester. Take exit 7 off I-93 onto Route 101 East. Take exit 1 off Route 101 and head south on Route 28. Proceed around a rotary and turn left into a parking lot at Lake Massabesic. *Directions to the eastern terminus:* Take Route 108 about a half-mile north of the junction with Route 85 and head toward Durham. Turn left onto unmarked Ash Swamp Road. Park at the abandoned railroad depot.

Once part of the Boston & Maine Railroad network, the Rockingham Recreational Trail runs east of Manchester to within a few miles of the Atlantic Ocean. All-terrain vehicles (ATVs) are permitted on the trail, so if you want the best chance of avoiding them, go on a weekday. From the west, the trail hugs the shoreline of Lake Massabesic. When you reach the 5-mile mark, you'll go through the first of the three short tunnels along the route. You'll soon approach Onway Lake. Enter through a granite corridor and the second tunnel before you reach Raymond. Congratulations, you've made it halfway. Now cross a sizable railroad bridge and you'll soon be accompanied by the Lamprey River. Traverse a few country roads until you find the town of Epping. The final 2 miles of the trail, past Newfields, is a peaceful jaunt through fields, eventually leading to an abandoned railroad station.

Kennebunk Bridle Path, New Hampshire. *Distance:* 5.6 miles (round-trip). *Time:* 45 minutes. *Difficulty:* Easy. *Directions:* From Kennebunk, head southeast on Route 35. When you see Tom's of Maine on your right, take the next right onto Sea Road and continue for 0.3 mile. Turn right into the parking lot of Sea Road School.

This short abandoned rail line is now used as a community path in the Kennebunk area. Parallel to the Mousam River, the ride is flat and is bordered on both sides by the Rachel Carson National Wildlife Refuge. It's a great first ride for young children who want to venture off-road. It's also a good ride for anyone who wants to escape the traffic of southern Maine. Turn right onto a trail that cuts through the school driveway. Two miles later, be cautious as you cross Route 9. The trail ends on Sea Road across from a golf course. Simply head back and do the ride as many times as your body craves.

Road Biking

Portsmouth Ramble, New Hampshire. *Distance:* 33 miles (loop). *Time:* 4 to 5 hours. *Difficulty:* Easy to moderate. *Directions:* Follow the small strawberry signs from Routes 1 and I-95 into the city of Portsmouth. Park in the municipal lot near Prescott Park.

Portsmouth's historic Strawbery Banke section is the start of this route that takes you inland before hugging Route 1A along the Atlantic coast. Traffic here is unrelenting in the summer, so try this ride in the spring or fall. From the parking lot, turn left onto narrow Marcy Street.

Thirty historic buildings make up this section of Portsmouth, dating as far back as the late 17th century. Turn right at a four-way intersection onto South Street and at the 1-mile mark turn left onto Route 1A (Sagamore Road). This is a residential neighborhood and traffic can be dense, but Route 1A is a wide two-lane road.

At 4.2 miles, bear right toward Rye Center. Bike for another 1.1 miles before bearing right at Washington Road and passing the Rye School. In Rye, woods and salt marsh surround the country estates that line the road. Cross Route 1 and continue for another 1.8 miles to a stop sign, just beyond the I-95 overpass. Turn left onto Route 151 for 2.4 miles before crossing over I-95 again and heading east. Turn left onto North Road. When you reach the junction of Route 1, turn left and immediately right, back onto North Street. Bike for 2 more miles to Woodland Road, turn right, and ride for another 1.5 miles to the junction of Route 111.

As you turn left onto Route 111, you'll start to smell the salty air of the sea. Then, 1.2 miles later, you'll reach Route 1A at Little Boars Head. Turn left for the highlight of the ride, a 10-mile stretch along the seashore. You'll pass mansions with their manicured lawns, antique shops, the beaches of Rye Harbor State Park and Wallis Sands State Beach (both are ideal for picnicking), and the walking trails of Odiorne Point State Park (see "Walks and Rambles"). Continue on Route 1A as it turns right and travel half a mile. Then turn right again onto Route 1B. Hug the coast for another 4.5 miles as you pass such historic sites as Wentworth-by-the-Sea, a late-19th-century hotel. Route 1B ends at Marcy Street, where you simply veer right to return to your car.

Walks and Rambles

Odiorne Point State Park, New Hampshire. *Distance:* 2 miles (loop). *Time:* 1 hour. *Difficulty:* Easy. *Directions:* From Portsmouth, take Route

1 to the Elwyn Road lights (Route 1A) and turn left. Follow Route 1A to the park entrance.

Situated at the far end of Portsmouth Harbor, Odiorne Point officially became a state park in 1972. This loop along the coast is a favorite of walkers, joggers, and birdwatchers. The trail takes you on Pebble Beach before heading inland through marsh and low-lying shrubs. Compared with the honky-tonk beaches in the state, this peaceful retreat is the perfect place for being at the ocean without the crowds.

Great Bay National Wildlife Refuge, New Hampshire. *Distance:* 2 miles (loop). *Time:* 1 hour. *Difficulty:* Easy. *Directions:* From the Spaulding Turnpike, 3 miles west of Portsmouth, take the Pease International Tradeport exit. Continue on Merrimac Road to McIntyre Road and you'll see a sign to enter Great Bay National Wildlife Refuge.

Formerly Pease Air Force Base, Great Bay is now the state's largest refuge, with more than 6 miles of bay shore. The sweeping bay has over 48 miles of coastline, beckoning a variety of birds that migrate along the Atlantic Flyway (see "Birding"). Take the 2-mile Ferry Way Trail through the woods, where you may be lucky enough to spot a wild turkey. Meander past small beaver ponds and an old apple orchard before heading down toward the shores of Great Bay. Then take the loop back to the parking lot.

Marginal Way, Ogunquit, Maine. *Distance:* 1.25 miles. *Time:* 1 hour. *Difficulty:* Easy. *Directions:* The trail leaves from Shore Road, off Route 1A, south of the town of Ogunquit.

Ogunquit gives walkers a first glimpse of Maine's rocky shores. This walk along the cliffs on granite headlands connects downtown with picturesque Perkins Cove. Ogunquit is a fishing village that has become a haven for artists, though lobster boats still work here and

Winslow Homer's Cliff Walk at Prout's Neck

there is fresh seafood to eat. Cross the footbridge and take a 20-minute walk along Shore Road back to the village. If you don't feel like walking back, you can always take the trolley. Just listen for the bell.

Cliff Walk, Prouts Neck, Maine. *Distance:* 1 mile (one way). *Time:* 45 minutes. *Difficulty:* Easy. *Directions:* Take I-96 to exit 6 (Scarborough). Turn left onto Payne Road and drive to the second light, turning right onto Route 114. This will take you all the way through Scarborough. When Route 114 veers left, continue straight to Route 207 (Black Point Road), which will take you to the cliffs of Prouts Neck and to Winslow Homer Road.

The small town of Prouts Neck has changed little since Winslow Homer painted every nook and cranny of these shores from 1883 to 1909. Outside Homer's studio, which is open to the public (Winslow Homer Road, Prouts Neck; open daily May through October, 10–5), juniper trees, planted by Homer, slope down from his backyard to the moors, eventually reaching the jagged gray Maine rock that lines most of the Neck's shoreline, detritus from a glacier that retreated more than 10,000 years ago. Then there's the great expanse of ocean where, in the distance, a mile or two out to sea, stand Bluff and Stratten Islands. Whitecap after whitecap come crashing into the rocks as if marching to their death.

The rugged scenery can best be appreciated by taking the mile-long Cliff Walk created by Homer's brother, Charles, in 1879. The broad Marginal Way was formed around the perimeter of the loop to preserve the most scenic part of the peninsula. To this day, the Prouts Neck Association has kept this area free of houses. The public is welcome to take the same walk Winslow Homer took almost every morning at 4:30 with his dog, Sam, a white wire-haired terrier. Often these strolls would be exploratory, a research-gathering expedition for Homer to learn more about the rocky coastline and how waves, wind, and shore interact. Ever so slowly, he came to know every rock, cliff, and bush on this varied shore and how they responded to the tumultuous Maine weather.

With the sounds of waves ringing in your ears, walk to the eastern part of the Neck. Bay, juniper, and huckleberry bushes line the Cliff Walk, dwarfed by the perennial blast of wind. First stop is **Cannon Rock,** where a formation resembling a small cannon juts out of the cliffside. Waves slam into the rocks and then flush down a foamy whirlpool back to sea, as Homer depicted in *Cannon Rock* (1895).

Continuing eastward, the Cliff Walk begins to climb, eventually reaching an old stone tower, called Seagate. Here the striated cliffs hover above the sea, offering exquisite views of the entire Neck. Homer aptly called this point **High Cliff** as seen in *High Cliff, Coast of Maine* (1894). This is the most dramatic section of shoreline, where breakers roll in with tremendous force against a wall of rock.

The Cliff Walk gradually descends, crossing a small wooden bridge, to reach **Kettle Cove.** At this shallow bay, site of hundreds of boulders, Homer created his final painting, *Driftwood* (1909). In his recurring theme of man facing the elements, a fisherman dressed in oilskins and a sou'wester hat struggles with a huge log in a storm. When Homer finished this work, he deliberately messed up the paints on his palette and hung it on the wall of his studio. This was his way of retiring.

Eastern Point, the final stop on the Cliff Walk, lies at the end of a rocky beach. Just offshore, a blackened ledge called **Black Rock** stands firm against the perpetual battering of surf. In one of his most famous paintings of the 1900s, *Eastern Point, Prouts Neck* (1900), Homer shows a churning wave shooting upward from Black Rock, practically touching the top of the canvas.

Continue your tour of Prouts Neck inland, on Winslow Homer Road, and turn right at a small trail sign that reads PNA SANCTUARY (Prout's Neck Association). Not only did Charles donate the Cliff Walk to the people of Prouts Neck, but he also gave about 15 acres of forest to provide a park for its residents. Take the Center Path into the woods, and within moments you're far away from the angry ocean, deep in a forest of old-growth pines. When you tire of hearing the songs of white-crowned sparrows coming from the branches, continue down the road back to Homer's studio.

TWO, IF BY SEA

Canoeing

Estes Lake, Sanford, Maine. *Distance:* 3–4 miles. *Time:* 2 to 3 hours. *Difficulty:* Easy. *Directions:* From the intersection of Routes 4, 4A, 111, and 202 in Alfred, drive south on Route 4 for 0.8 mile past that junction, then veer left on unmarked Bernier Road. After another 0.8 mile you'll find the put-in beside a tiny bridge.

It's unusual to find several miles of undeveloped shoreline on a lake in southern Maine, but that's exactly what you get at Estes. About 10 miles inland from Wells and less than an hour's drive from Portland, 4-mile-long Estes Lake offers a good half-day of paddling.

From Hay Brook, paddle east past the swamp maples and alders. Blue herons and mallards hang out on the shores. Veer right to enter the main body of the lake. You can paddle for an hour and then head back to Hay Brook or continue south to the more populated shores of the lake. Steer well clear of the dam that created this body of water and you'll spot a trio of rocky islands that are a perfect place for lunch.

Fishing

Surf-cast on the coast from May through September for stripers, while bluefish peak in August. If you have a boat, head up the Piscataqua River on the border between New Hampshire and Maine, where the rip is big, deep, and hard flowing.

For charters, contact the **Atlantic Fleet** (Rye Harbor Marina, State Route 1A, Rye; 603-964-5220) to cast for saltwater fish. Anglers on this outfit's 70-foot party boat reel in cod, pollock, and haddock. In Hampton Beach, **Smith & Gilmore** (603-926-3503) offers deep-sea fishing trips off the coast of New Hampshire and into the Gulf of Maine for cod, haddock, pollock, striped bass, and bluefish. On Maine's south coast at Ogunquit, Captain Tim Tower offers full- and half-day trips on the ***Bunny Clark*** (207-646-2214).

Scuba Diving

If you have your own gear and want to check out the New Hampshire coast, open the diving web site of the **University of New Hampshire** (http://nemo.unh.edu/aqualung/nhdive_home.htm). The page names the best places along the coast to dive and what you'll find once you get there. You can also dive with seals and find wrecks with **York Beach Scuba** (Railroad Avenue, York Beach, Maine; 207-363-3330).

Sea Kayaking

Portsmouth Kayak Adventures (603-559-1000; www.portsmouth kayak.com) offers paddlers a choice of tours—from an ocean kayak journey around the Isle of Shoals to an inland excursion on Great Bay. Great Bay is a vast estuary where salt water and fresh water meet to create an Eden for birds and fish (see "Birding"). The five-hour Isle of Shoals tour begins in Portsmouth Harbor and goes to Gosport Harbor, 7 miles off the coast. As you kayak, you will hear about the history of each of the nine partially submerged islands that make up the Isle of Shoals, once home to a wild contingent of poets, painters, and pirates.

North of Portsmouth, southern Maine's **Scarborough Marsh** is a 3,100-acre estuary of fresh water and salt water full of bird life, including the purple glossy ibis. The Maine Audubon Society operates a nature center here, with canoe rentals. Sea kayaking might be preferable, however, since the 10-foot tide and strong winds are a challenge inside a canoe. Paddle out against the tide while you're still feeling strong and that same tide will help carry you back in. Stick to main river channels in order to not get caught in narrow inlets when the tide goes out. To reach Scarborough Marsh from Portland, take Route 1 South and turn left on Route 9 toward Pine Point. Drive 0.8 mile to the nature center on the left.

Then there's the following jaunt outside the city of Portland.

Casco Bay Islands, Portland. *Distance:* 3–4 miles. *Time:* 4 hours.

Difficulty: Moderate. *Directions:* To get to Peaks Island in the Casco Bay Islands for the start of this kayak trip, board the Casco Bay Lines vessel that leaves every hour in the summer from Portland for the 20-minute voyage.

Portland's four centuries of seagoing heritage endures, but now it's seasoned with big-city refugees from Boston and New York who want to live by the ocean in a close-knit community of some 65,000. Like most American waterfronts, the Old Port district of the city has been gentrified. Rotting wharves and empty warehouses on Commercial Street have been converted into condominiums, and the red-brick Victorian buildings on Exchange and Middle Streets have been transformed into boutiques, office space, and restaurants. Yet when the rush of commercial development came close to washing out this working waterfront in one big 1980s' tsunami, the people of Portland decided to protect and rebuild the city's dilapidated fish pier. Today, the Portland Fish Exchange is a thriving fish auction and the Port of Portland handles the largest volume of fresh seafood in the Northeast.

While lobstermen ply the ocean waters for their catch, Portland executives play in the ocean with their shiny new kayaks. You can paddle around a few of the 220 Casco Bay Islands (only a quarter of them are inhabited) with **Maine Island Kayak Company** (1-800-796-2373; www.sea-kayak.com) for full-day paddles ($90) or half-day paddles ($55).

Water temperature was a cool 54 degrees Fahrenheit with winds at 10 knots out of the northwest as we slid into our boats and paddled over to Fort Gorges, built just before the Civil War. The seas were relatively calm as we passed several lobstermen who were busy chucking out the smaller crustaceans that didn't make minimum weight.

From atop the thick stone walls of the fort, we could see the Portland waterfront in all its rugged grandeur. Huge cranes were fixing the larger boats of the fleet while oil storage tanks mushroomed silver along the wharves.

Back in our kayaks, we fought a tough headwind as we made our way around the northern tip of Great Diamond Island. Ospreys nested in the tall pines that lined the granite shores. Farther inland, new houses were being built to accommodate more year-round commuters who yearn to have the sea as their welcome mat.

Surfing

Surfing nirvana can sometimes be found at The Wall at North Beach in Hampton, New Hampshire. For surfing news daily, contact **Cinnamon Rainbows** (603-926-WAVE) or visit their surf shack at 931 Ocean Boulevard, North Beach, Hampton.

A DAY AT THE BEACH

New Hampshire has 18 miles of Atlantic Coast shoreline, complete with large stretches of beach, dunes, and saltwater marshes. The ocean can be a wee bit on the chilly side (60 degrees seems about the norm), but the sun will make your body toasty in the summer months, so any body of water will do nicely, thank you.

Hampton Beach State Park is still the place to go for families, college kids, and everybody else who relishes a boisterous crowd. On summer weekends, come early to find a spot for your beach towel amid the thousands. Activity still focuses around the century-old casino, which features restaurants, penny arcades, shops, and a nightclub.

To the south, **Seabrook Beach** is in a heavily developed residential area with little public access to the ocean since parking is limited. **North Hampton Beach** is a good place to stroll past the old fish houses, which are now summer cottages.

A sidewalk follows the coast for some 2 miles to the Rye Beach Club. But **Jenness Beach** and **Wallis Sands State Beach** in Rye, north of Hampton Beach, are far more accessible, with a wide crescent of sand and ample parking. They tend to be a little more laid-back than Hampton, but with so little shoreline in the state, all the beaches are on-the-beaten-track.

For the only undeveloped strip of New Hampshire coastline, head to **Odiorne Point State Park** in Portsmouth.

The broad, flat southern Maine beaches are great for strolling, jogging, or plain ole tanning. **Long Sands Beach** in York is a mile and a half long and stretches between York Harbor and the Nubble, with views of Nubble Lighthouse. The surf is good here, so this is a decent place to ride the waves.

Ogunquit's **Main Beach** is off Beach Street in town. The 3 miles of flat white sand are a favorite tourist attraction. To escape the crowds, head 2 miles north of Main Beach on Ocean Street and turn right to reach the **Footbridge Beach** parking lot. This section of Ogunquit's shoreline is far less congested.

The 7-mile-long strip of sand at **Wells Beach** is flanked by the ocean on one side and salt marsh on the other. Wide, the beach offers plenty of elbow room for sun lovers. **Goose Rocks Beach** near Kennebunkport features two broad crescent-shaped beaches stretching for 3 miles. The gently lapping waves and wading pools left by the receding tide make it ideal for families.

Then there's the legendary 7-mile-long, 700-foot-wide **Old Orchard Beach,** with amusement park, pier, and other honky-tonk attractions. For a little more intimacy, try **Fortune Rocks Beach** near Biddeford Pool and **Laudholm Beach** off Laudholm Road in Elms.

CAMPGROUNDS

Tidewater Campground, Hampton, New Hampshire (603-926-5474). From the junction of Route 1 and Route 101 in Hampton, head south on Route 1 for 0.25 mile. The entrance is on the right-hand side. The campground provides 225 sites (175 with water and electric hook-ups), metered hot showers, rest rooms, a rec hall, a playground, and a small store. This RV park puts you 2 miles east of Hampton Beach. Anglers can head south to the Hampton State Pier, right before the Seabrook Bridge.

Salty Acres Campground, Kennebunkport, Maine (207-967-2483). From the junction of Routes 9A/35 and Route 9, head 5 miles east on Route 9 to the campground. There are 400 sites (70 with full hook-ups; 90 with water and electric), hot showers, flush toilets, picnic tables, a swimming pool, a playground, and a store. This large campground is conveniently located on the coast, near the stores of Kennebunkport and the sands of Goose Rocks Beach. Head to Kennebunkport Harbor to inquire about fishing and boating charters.

Shamrock RV Park, Biddeford, Maine (207-284-4282). From the junction of Routes 1, 111, and West Street in downtown Biddeford, drive 4.5 miles east on West Street to the campground. Here are 60 sites (25 with full hook-ups; 19 with water and electric), hot showers, flush toilets, picnic tables, a swimming pool, a playground, and a store. This peaceful spot in a rural area is near Biddeford Pools and Fortune Rocks Beach.

CHAPTER SIX
Maine

▶ In 1910, two men from Harvard, Dr. Charles Eliot and George Buckman Dorr, were so enraged that lumber companies were cutting down Mount Desert Island's first-growth forest that they decided to do something that would have a lasting impression on the Maine landscape. They called on their wealthy friends and raised enough money to buy about 15,000 acres on Mount Desert—one-fifth of the island. Today the Park makes up roughly half of the island. The men then donated the land to the U.S. government to create the first national park this side of the Mississippi. In 1919, the place was officially named Lafayette National Park, but ten years later the name was changed to Acadia National Park. Other rich patrons soon did their part. John D. Rockefeller Jr. offered 43 miles of bridle paths. The owners of nearby Isle au Haut gave the southern half of the island in 1943 to complete Acadia's total of 47,633 acres.

Acadia is just one of the gems of the Maine coast. The entire Maine shore north of Portland now constitutes one of the most desired coastlines in America. Travelers from all over the world come to bike the remote Penobscot Bay islands. Hikers venture here for the opportunity to climb Cadillac Mountain, the highest mountain directly on the East Coast (1,530 feet). Sea kayakers and sailors navigate around the fingers of land that, on a map of the coast, hang down from the shoreline like icicles. Walkers and birdwatchers flock to the coast to spot bald eagles, peregrine falcons, even puffins. Mountain bikers, rock climbers, and scuba divers are all challenged by Acadia National Park. Throw the gear in the trunk and pick a coastal adventure.

THE TERRAIN

North of Portland, the sand is gone, replaced by a long coastline of rock, grooved and roughened by the endless battering of surf and wind. This is the ragged Maine coast that has lured fishermen, shipbuilders, and artists for centuries.

At Acadia National Park's Mount Desert Island, granite mountains rise 1,500 feet above the water's edge. Glaciers rounded the summits and dug out the floors of the valley into U-shaped troughs. These basins now contain freshwater lakes and New England's only fjord, Somes Sound.

Some four thousand years ago, lichens, mosses, and other simple plant life covered the rocks with a thin layer of vegetation. The birches crept forward from the south, followed by pines, spruces, firs, and the slower-growing oaks and maples. Today the northern Maine coast is a picturesque combination of forest, sea, and rock.

GETTING HERE

The Maine coastline is long: from Portland in the south to Eastport, not far from Canada, is a distance of 293 miles. With the peninsulas, and the winding shoreline that looks like it was created from the scribbles of a five-year-old, you have a drive that takes six or seven hours. Interstate 95, the Maine Turnpike, will take you as far north as

Brunswick before heading inland. If you're traveling to Acadia National Park, you can just stay on I-95 to Bangor and then go south on Route 3. But if you want to stay near the coast north of Brunswick, drive up Route 1, often a two-lane highway, as it meanders from seaside village to seaside village.

Many visitors begin their trip up the Maine coast with a stop at the mammoth L.L. Bean store in Freeport (1-800-341-4341), 16 miles north of Portland. The 24-hour store, run by the company that was created more than a century ago by Leon Leonwood Bean, has become a big attraction, selling almost any gear or clothing you could possibly need to enjoy Maine's great outdoors.

The coast is known for its dense fog, which can cool things off in the summer and fall. The best time to visit Acadia and points north is mid-August when the bugs are gone, the blueberries are ripe, and the temperatures are in the high 70s.

The Activities

ONE, IF BY LAND

Birding

The Maine coast and its islands are proven pit stops for migrating shorebirds, particularly the larger varieties, like herons and marsh hawks. Bald eagles can be seen at **Quoddy State Park** (see "Walks and Rambles"), and peregrine falcons nest in **Acadia National Park** (see the Champlain Mountain entry under "Hiking"). In Georgetown, the 119-acre **Josephine Newman Sanctuary** features more than 60 bird species, including the barred owl, great blue heron, snowy egret, and American goldfinch. The sanctuary lies off Route 127, 9 miles south of its junction with Route 1 in Woolwich (which is about 35 miles northeast of Portland). The park is on the right-hand side of the road just past the post office in Georgetown. Head down the gravel road and park at the end.

Machias Seal Island is a highlight for birders—a tiny unspoiled sanctuary near the mouth of the Bay of Fundy for some of Maine's most noted marine bird species. You can visit the island via a charter boat, such as the *Barbara Frost* that operates out of Cutler. To reach the *Barbara Frost* (207-259-4484), take Route 1 East to East Machias on the northeastern Maine coast and turn right onto Route 191 South to Cutler. Park across from the white Methodist church. Arrive at 7 AM for the 9-mile cruise to Machias Seal Island.

From Cutler, you'll soon be gliding past lobster boats and circular salmon-farming nets as you cruise out of the harbor and into the Atlantic. This is the Maine shoreline north of Bar Harbor, where summer estates are replaced by lighthouses that warn boaters of its unmerciful tides and harsh coast. An hour later you will disembark onto small, low-lying Machias Seal Island. Hundreds of plump birds may whiz over your head as they search the waters for breakfast. One of the bird species has a black head that makes it look like Batman; this is the razorbill auk. Another has wide eyes and a beak dotted red, black, and yellow. This is the bird everyone is excited to see: the Atlantic puffin.

Machias Seal Island is the southernmost major nesting site of these stubby penguinlike birds. Small colonies of Atlantic puffins have been reestablished farther south by the National Audubon Society, but those puffins can be viewed only from the sea. At Machias, weather permitting, you can climb atop the seaweed-slick rocks and see puffins two to three feet away.

The eastern part of the island is covered with Arctic terns. The

Machias Seal Island

razorbill auk might look like a superhero, but it is the aggressive tern that keeps deadly predators like seagulls away from the eggs of all the island's birds. Harassment by gulls is a major problem in many of the puffin colonies. A puffin returning to its nest with several capelin dangling from its bill might be forced to drop the fish in order to escape from gull abuse. Gulls have also been known to eat chicks that stray from their parents' watch. The puffins are greatly indebted to the terns for their watchfulness; stray off the island's main path and you might hear the irate click-click-clicking of a fearless tern one foot above your head. Paths lead to four blinds where you can set up shop and watch the puffins. You might also find yellow-crowned night herons and several kinds of swallows.

You are allowed up to three hours on the island before your return to Cutler. On the return trip, you will glide around a small hump of land known as **Gull Island.** This is a playground for harbor seals,

187

whose heads can be seen bobbing up and down with the waves.

The round-trip from Cutler takes five to six hours, and you should reserve well in advance since there is a limit on the number of people allowed on Machias Seal Island. The *Barbara Frost* is operated by Bold Coast Charter Company (207-259-4484; www.boldcoast.com). The *Barbara Frost* also offers half-day and full-day trips to **Cross Island Wildlife Refuge,** a site near Cutler that is ideal for birding and picnicking. Several boats make the trip to Machias Seal Island from Jonesport, Maine; you can contact **Captain Barna B. Norton** in Jonesport at 207-497-5933.

Golf

With 13 holes bordering Penobscot Bay and its very own lighthouse, the **Samoset Golf Course** in Rockport (207-594-1431) is coastal Maine's perennial favorite. Situated on the resort of the same name, the front 9 makes the most of the ocean view, while the back 9 meanders through woods, ponds, and gardens. Hole number 7, the course's signature hole, is a par-5 dogleg left that practically dares you to play over the ocean. Don't mind the brisk breeze.

The **Kebo Valley Golf Club** on Eagle Lake in Bar Harbor (207-288-3000), with a course laid out in 1888, provides a challenging links-type course in the north woods—a great place during fall foliage.

Hiking

Finally, some mountains to climb on the New England coast! Maine's coastal mountains reward hikers with views of the surrounding hills, ocean, and lakes in exchange for one or two hours of effort.

Mount Battie, near Camden. *Distance:* 1 mile (round-trip). *Time:* 1 hour. *Difficulty:* Moderate. *Directions:* Take Route 52 North from its

The view from atop Mount Battie

intersection with Route 1 in Camden. Turn right at the first street from the intersection, then turn left on Megunticook Street. Park in the small lot at the top of the hill.

The ascent to the summit of Mount Battie takes only 30 minutes, but you should be in good condition, because the trail climbs up steep rocks the entire way. Once on top, you'll enjoy a commanding view. Camden's white steeples and schooners' masts surge to the sky, surrounded by the ubiquitous pine. The island of North Haven lies straight ahead, Islesboro to the left, and Matinicus to the right. Climb up the tower to get an even better view, and then make your way slowly back down.

Maiden Cliff, near Camden. *Distance:* 2.25 miles (round-trip). *Time:* 2 hours. *Difficulty:* Easy. *Directions:* From Camden, take Route 52 West, 3 miles from the intersection of Route 1. You'll find a small parking area on the right side of the road just before Route 52 borders the lake.

The view from Champlain Mountain

This trail starts gradually, slowly climbing through the hemlocks until you reach a junction at the half-mile mark. Turn right onto Ridge Trail and soon the ledges open up onto a view of the waters of Megunticook Lake. The view only gets better as you turn left at the Scenic Trail and continue to climb. Camden and Penobscot Bay can be seen in the distance. However, this is not the Maiden Cliff. To get there, walk downhill and follow the white blazes until you reach a junction, where you'll turn right. A couple hundred yards later, you'll find a huge white cross atop Maiden Cliff overlooking all of Megunticook Lake. The wooden cross marks the spot where 12-year-old Elenora French plunged to her death on May 7, 1864, as she was running to catch her hat. This might be the fastest way down, but I suggest taking the Maiden Cliff trail directly back to the parking lot.

Acadia Mountain, on Mount Desert Island. *Distance:* 2 miles (round-trip). *Time:* 1 to 2 hours. *Difficulty:* Easy. *Directions:* From Bar Harbor take Route 233 west to Somesville. The trailhead is located 3 miles south of Somesville on Route 102. Park at the small lot where the Acadia Mountain sign is clearly hung.

The path to Acadia Mountain starts on the other side of Route 102. A mere 681 feet high, Acadia Mountain overlooks much of Mount Desert Island. The trail is situated on the island's far less congested western side, where you'll rarely see more than a handful of hikers even in midsummer. The path weaves slowly through forests of birch and pine before crossing a former road. The quick ascent to the summit begins here.

A series of flat ledges look over Echo Lake—each step offering a better view than the last. Before you can swat that incredibly annoying black fly, you're the next Edmund Hillary. As you cross over the rocks, the view becomes sensational. The Cranberry Islands look like peas in a pod, while numerous yachts are safely anchored in Southwest Harbor. Proceed to the easternmost point of Acadia's peak for the finest view: Norumbega Mountain practically collapses into Somes Sound, the only fjord on the eastern seaboard. (A fjord happens when a wall of rock precipitously drops off into a glacially carved deep trough. Mountains are necessary to create a fjord—thus, the reason this only occurs in this part of the eastern seaboard.)

Champlain Mountain, on Mount Desert Island. *Distance:* 4.4 miles (round-trip). *Time:* 2 hours. *Difficulty:* Moderate. *Directions:* From the Acadia National Park Visitor Center, take the Park Loop to the Bear Brook Trail sign. There are several parking places across the street.

The Bear Brook Trail to the summit of Champlain Mountain is one of those amazing climbs where you are always spinning around to see the view behind you. In this case, the view is of the expansive Frenchman Bay. With every step upward, there seems to be yet another green spot below you that adds to a line of islands.

The climb to the 1,058-foot peak is not effortless. The ascent is on a rocky path. At the 1.1-mile mark, you can see a small island ahead called The Thumbcap, the lighthouse on Egg Rock, the town of Bar Harbor, and a tiny pond to your left known as The Tarn. You may discover that the Precipice Trail to the top is closed in summer to protect nesting peregrine falcons. A good place to spot these swift birds is from the Precipice Trail parking lot on the Park Loop, less than a mile from where your car is parked.

Horseback Riding

Ledgewood Riding Stables (207-882-6346), near Boothbay Harbor, offers one- and two-hour wooded trail rides for ages seven and older. The ride snakes into a forest where, if you are lucky, you might spot a deer or even a moose.

Mountain Biking

Carriage Path Trails, Acadia National Park. *Distance:* 14 miles (loop). *Time:* 2 hours. *Difficulty:* Easy. *Directions:* Start at the Visitor Center off Route 3.

The carriage path trails in Acadia National Park are not mountain biking paths in the classic sense of the word—no exhilarating single-track rides down Cadillac Mountain. Instead, the trails are hard-packed gravel, better suited to the fat wheels of a mountain bike than the narrow wheels of a road bike. Donated to the park by John D. Rockefeller Jr., this 43-mile network of trails traverses the entire eastern half of Mount Desert Island. The trails are off-limits to motorized vehicles, and thus are the best way to see this part of Acadia by two wheels.

Among the routes is this 14-mile loop that makes a worthy introduction to these trails. Start at the northern end of the Visitor Center parking lot, where there's a dirt path and a small bicycle sign. The next half-mile is the toughest part of the entire ride, an unrelenting uphill climb. At signpost 1, bear left, then take another left at signpost 3. This will bring you past placid Witch Hole Pond to a stone arched bridge high above roaring Duck Brook.

Take a quick look from the overview, but continue riding along the same trail. Bear left at signpost 4 and ride downhill under a stone bridge to the shores of Eagle Lake, Acadia's second-largest body of water. Circle the lake counterclockwise in the forest of pines. The steady uphill climb at the southern part of the lake will reward you with a dramatic view of Cadillac Mountain as you speed downhill toward the lake's eastern shores.

At signpost 9, turn right under the stone bridge again and take a left at signpost 4. This will give you an even better view of Witch Hole Pond. Two more lefts, at signpost 2 and signpost 1, will bring you back to the Visitor Center parking lot.

Road Biking

Just above Portland, fingers of land, some more than 20 miles long, reach out into the Atlantic off Route 1. Estuaries, coves, and fishing villages beckon bikers to this remote coastline. Even more isolated are the Penobscot Bay islands, where ferries provide the only way to enter and leave. Even during midsummer, traffic here is at a crawl.

Rockport-Camden-Megunticook Lake, near Camden. *Distance:* 20 miles (round-trip). *Time:* 3 hours. *Difficulty:* Moderate to strenuous. *Terrain:* Hilly. *Directions:* From Route 1 just south of Camden, veer east on Main Street to get to downtown Rockport. There will be a clearly marked sign to Rockport Center.

The roads around Camden Hills State Park are a must for local bik-

A lighthouse in the Penobscot Bay Islands

ers, but be ready: The gently rolling terrain can suddenly turn into strenuous uphill climbs that will have your legs yearning for the long downhill run. This loop starts at Mary-Lea Park, overlooking Rockport's picturesque harbor.

Begin on Central Avenue and go up the hill, turning right on Russell Avenue. Soon Lily Pond will appear, along with peculiar-looking black cows with circular white stripes across their bellies. These designer cows are better known as belted Galloways.

Rural Russell Avenue soon changes into crowded Chestnut Street as you approach Camden. Veer left at the stone church and then bear right onto Route 1, being wary of the traffic. Take a sharp left onto Route 105 West for your first uphill struggle. On the right, Megunticook Lake soon materializes, along with Maiden Cliff and the other Camden hills rising from the far shores.

The route continues around Megunticook Lake as you turn right onto Route 235 North (Willey Corner Road). This shady road passes through the small farming village of Lincolnville. Turn right onto Route 52 South when you hit the stop sign. At Youngstown Inn, the road curves downhill, hugging the eastern shores of Megunticook Lake.

The trail starts here for Maiden Cliff (see "Hiking"), where you can get a bird's-eye view of the lake you just circled. The bike ride continues on Route 52 South. Bear right on Route 1 to enter the heart of Camden. If you can resist the lure of the galleries, shops, and chowder houses that line the downtown streets, bear left on Chestnut Street and retrace your way to Rockport.

Islesboro, near Camden. *Distance:* 28 miles (loop). *Time:* 3 to 4 hours. *Difficulty:* Easy to moderate. *Terrain:* Relatively flat. *Directions:* Take the ferry to the island of Islesboro from Lincolnville, which is 5 miles north of Camden. Contact the Maine State Ferry Service at 207-789-5611 or 207-734-6935.

The Penobscot Bay Islands offer some of the best biking in the Northeast. On the ferry ride over, bikers of all ages stand on deck, ready and rarin' to go. The island of Islesboro is relatively flat, yet hilly enough to offer exquisite views of the bay and big enough to offer a 28-mile bike ride.

Disembark and ride straight on the only road from the ferry. Your first right leads to a T-intersection, where you turn right again. This is Main Street, which passes the million-dollar mansions (so-called "summer cottages") of Dark Harbor on the way south to Pendleton Point. At the point, the perennial battering of the surf has exposed long, striated rocks that look like rotted tree trunks. Harbor seals and loons usually lounge in the water while you rest on the rocks.

After visiting Pendleton Point, turn around and make your way back to Dark Harbor, veering left on the road just before the general store—one of the few places on the island to buy lunch. This short road loops around secluded shoreline estates before turning left and back onto Main Street. As you head north, the road narrows, offering views of Camden Hills State Park to the left and the numerous islands of Penobscot Bay to the right.

Main Street forks a half-mile out. Veer left and pedal up a grueling hill, from which you can see sailboats in the distant bay, and then zip downhill on an exhilarating run through an opening in an ocean seawall. The road loops around the northern tip of the island past small farms, eventually curving downhill to Durkee's General Store and Main Street again. Turn right just past the Islesboro Historical Society building for more views of the shoreline before turning right onto Ferry Road.

North Haven, near Rockland. *Distance:* 20 miles (loop). *Time:* 3 hours. *Difficulty:* Moderate. *Terrain:* Hilly. *Directions:* Take the ferry from Rockland to the island of North Haven. Contact the Maine State Ferry Service for times; 207-596-2203.

The rustic countryside of North Haven seems much less populated than that of Islesboro. This loop begins at the ferry landing, veers left onto Main Street, and proceeds up the hill by the post office. At the 1.5-mile mark, take a right at the fork onto South Shore Road. There are hardly any road signs on this island, but it's difficult to get lost. Wide-open vistas of this former sheep-grazing island stand before you, and in early June, fields of purple hyacinth are in bloom.

The road sweeps around the eastern end of the island, soon displaying views of the ocean. Yachts are anchored in a small harbor under a bridge—Pulpit Harbor. You'll soon find the Pulpit Harbor Inn, where you bear right onto Crabtree Point Road. Speed downhill until

Cycling Mount Desert Island

you can make the first right turn. One-third of a mile later, veer left onto a dirt road under a shady forest of pines. Don't be surprised to find deer on this section of the island.

Take a right, back onto Crabtree Point Road, which cruises downhill to a dirt path just beyond a rocky beach on your right. This is the turnaround point. With mountain views in the distance and glowing yellow lobster buoys floating closer to shore, the beach is an ideal place to picnic. Return on Crabtree Point Road and make a right at the Grange Hall. Another right on the next paved road brings you back to the Main Street ferry terminal.

Southwest Harbor Loop, Mount Desert Island. *Distance:* 28 miles (loop). *Time:* 3 to 5 hours. *Difficulty:* Moderate to strenuous. *Directions:* Start on Main Street in the village of Southwest Harbor, on Route 102.

The eastern side of Mount Desert Island is very popular during

July and August. If you want to escape the maddening crowds, try this ride around the western half of the island. Here you'll cruise past lakes, ponds, the Atlantic, pine mountains, and timeless fishing villages.

Begin in the village of Southwest Harbor, where stores providing lobster traps outnumber souvenir shops. Proceed onto Route 102 South along the harbor and bear left onto Route 102A. You will ride past **Manset,** best known for its yachtmaking, and **Seawall,** where a natural stone seawall juts into the Atlantic toward the Cranberry Islands. A fun excursion is the half-mile road to the left that introduces you to the **Bass Harbor Head lighthouse,** founded in 1858.

Continue on Route 102A into Bass Harbor, following the signs for the Swans Island Ferry. This slight detour will bring you to the ferry dock. If you feel like biking all day, try the 40-minute crossing to Swans Island, which contains 7 more remote miles of paved road.

To return to Route 102A, just zip downhill and make a left at the junction. At the next intersection bear left at the sign to Seal Cove onto Route 102 North. Ride through the villages of Bernard and West Tremont to the farming community of **Seal Cove.** This is the most arduous section of the route, up and down all the way to Pretty Marsh. Console yourself with views of Seal Cove and Hodgdon Ponds, remote water spots straight out of an Ansel Adams photo.

Soon you'll be at the northern edge of **Long Pond,** the largest lake in Acadia National Park. If you want to give your legs a break, rent a canoe across the street and try some paddling. Back on your bike, turn left at the T-intersection to see the oldest community on Mount Desert Island, **Somesville,** founded in 1761.

To return to Southwest Harbor, do an about-face and proceed south on Route 102. You'll see Echo Lake to the right. Turn left on Clark Point Road in town and rush to **Beal's Lobster Pier.** You may

Lobster traps in Jonesport

find that an order of lobster and steamers is an ample reward for completing this ride.

Jonesport, northeastern Maine coast. *Distance:* 30 miles (loop). *Time:* 3 to 4 hours. *Difficulty:* Moderate to strenuous. *Terrain:* Hilly. *Directions:* Take Route 1 North past Columbia Falls to a Rest Area, and park there. (If you enter Jonesboro, you've gone too far.)

North of Acadia National Park, Route 1 leaves behind the world of tourism and affords us a glimpse into the everyday life of rural Maine. Fishing villages and fields of blueberries replace the honky-tonk T-shirt shops and motels of southern Maine. This is the Sunrise Coast, where you can see the sun rise first in the U.S.

This is why you may want to embark on this loop as early as possible. At the Rest Area on Route 1, bear right from the parking lot. Watch out for the traffic on Route 1. At the 2.7-mile mark, turn right onto Route 187 South and relish this loop that will soon return you to

Route 1. This scenic circuit is bordered by dark blueberry barrens and large swaths of farmland.

Midway to Jonesport, the mighty Atlantic Ocean makes its presence known. The water accompanies you south until you reach Jonesport, the very definition of a Maine harbor town. Take the bridge to Beal's Island to see stacks of lobster traps, piled high on the docks, surrounded by fishing boats that look like they need a long rest. If you wish, you may extend your trip to Great Wass Island. Otherwise, turn back at the white Methodist church, crossing the bridge back to Jonesport. Bear left onto Route 187 again for a wavy ride back. At Route 1, make a right to return to the Rest Area.

Rock Climbing

Superior rock climbing may be Acadia National Park's best-kept secret. The same glacier-carved granite cliffs and faces that challenge expert climbers are also available to novices. The two most popular areas are Otter Cliffs, a 60-foot sea cliff, and the south wall of Champlain Mountain, 200 feet high, set in from the ocean but with incredible views.

Atlantic Climbing (24 Cottage Street, Bar Harbor; 207-288-2521) takes beginners for half-day classes to Otter Cliffs, a top-roping area with great climbs like *Wonderwall* (with the moderate rating of 5.6). It is also home to the epic *A Dare by the Sea* (rated at 5.10+). Among the less-crowded areas recommended by Atlantic Climbing are South Bubble and Great Head, another sea cliff.

Walks and Rambles

The following are a few of the many nature trails that dot the Maine coast and islands. You also may want to try the walks at **Josephine Newman Sanctuary** in Georgetown and **Isle au Haut's** Western Head and Cliff Trails, part of Acadia National Park.

Reid State Park, Georgetown. *Distance:* 5 to 6 miles. *Time:* 3 hours. *Difficulty:* Easy. *Directions:* From Route 1 in Woolwich (about 35 miles northeast of Portland), head south on Route 127 for 9.5 miles and bear sharply to the right. Another 3 miles along Harmon Harbor brings you to the park entrance. Keep left and park your car at the far left parking lot after about another quarter-mile.

Off the beaten track, this magical state park is well worth a detour off Route 1 for a walk or dip. From the parking lot, head down to the water toward **Griffith Head.** This high granite bluff rewards you with exquisite views of the entire Sheepscot Bay. After watching the lobstermen pick up their traps, head south along the dunes of One-Mile Beach. Cross a series of ledges to reach Half-Mile Beach. Even more remote than One-Mile, Half-Mile is bordered by wild roses in June. Turn right onto a paved road near the administration building. The road takes you 2.25 miles through marshland back to the park entrance and a quick right to your car.

Rockland Breakwater, at Rockland. *Distance:* 2.25 miles. *Time:* 30 minutes to 1 hour. *Difficulty:* Easy. *Directions:* From Rockland, take Route 1 North and turn right at Waldo Avenue. There will be a small sign for the Samoset Resort. Take a right on Samoset Road and park at the end.

If you want to feel like you're at the edge of the world, take this enjoyable walk to the **Rockland Lighthouse.** You'll be treated to a visual feast at sunset. On your right you can see schooners in the harbor; to your left, the mountains of Camden Hills State Park watch over Maine's jagged coastline. Jeeps used to be permitted on the stone jetty, resulting in large cracks, so be careful. Walk to the end of the breakwater to reach the lighthouse.

Monhegan Island, South Loop. *Distance:* 2 miles (round-trip). *Time:*

1 to 2 hours. *Difficulty:* Easy. *Directions:* Take the ferry to Monhegan Island from Port Clyde, Boothbay Harbor, or Damariscotta. From Port Clyde, call the Monhegan Boat Line at 207-372-8848. From Boothbay Harbor, call 207-633-2284. From Damariscotta, call 207-677-2026.

Monhegan Island has captivated artists for over a century. This trail originates at **Monhegan Spa,** just above the docks. Walk through the small village and head uphill on a gravel road that soon becomes grass-covered. Above the rocks of Lobster Cove, where good views highlight the mainland, a narrow path snakes its way east along the shores before climbing through a forest of balsam fir and spruce. You will begin to see the abstract rock formations in Gull Cove and the 160-foot-high cliffs at White Head. This is a fine place to eat and to absorb unbeatable views of the ocean. After this experience, take a left onto White Head Trail, a grass-covered road. As you return to Monhegan Spa, you'll pass the **Monhegan Lighthouse.**

Ocean Trail, Acadia National Park. *Distance:* 4 miles (round-trip). *Time:* 2 hours. *Difficulty:* Easy. *Directions:* From the Visitor Center, head south on Park Loop Road. After 3 miles, bear left as a sign directs you to Sand Beach. Continue for another 6 miles and turn left into the Sand Beach parking area. The Ocean Trail begins at the south end of the parking lot.

This wondrous trail hugs the shoreline, climbing over rocks and through pines to reach such Acadia National Park highlights as **Thunder Hole.** You will arrive at this narrow cut in the rock about 0.6 mile into the walk. The surf booms as it surges into the small channel. Continue on the bluffs past **Monument Cove,** a small beach covered with smooth rocks. A mile into the walk, the trail enters a fir and spruce forest, reaching Otter Point, then Otter Cove, 1 mile later.

Jordan Pond Trail, Acadia National Park. *Distance:* 3.3 miles (loop).

Time: 1 to 2 hours. *Difficulty:* Easy. *Directions:* From the Visitor Center, drive 8 miles south on Park Loop Road to the Jordan Pond parking area. The signed trail begins on the western side of the second parking lot. Walk a tenth of a mile to the shores of Jordan Pond.

Inevitably, folks think of the ocean when they picture Acadia National Park. Yet Acadia also features some of the most serene bodies of fresh water near the coast. This loop circles Jordan Pond, surrounded by a ring of mountains—Sargent, the Bubbles, Pemetic, and Penobscot. The varied trail passes through forests of birch and fir, a beach, and a wetland, which you cross on log bridges and boardwalks.

Quoddy Head State Park, on the northeastern coast. *Distance:* 4 miles. *Time:* 2 hours. *Difficulty:* Easy. *Directions:* From Lubec, turn left onto South Lubec Road and take the first left, onto Quoddy Head Road. You'll see a small sign and parking lot for Quoddy Head State Park on the right.

Quoddy Head State Park rests on the easternmost point of the United States, where Maine borders New Brunswick, Canada. Here, cliffs rise 90 to 150 feet, formed by the battering surf below. Take the short trail to the left, which leads to the red-and-white-banded Quoddy Head lighthouse, built in 1858. All of Grand Manan Island's 12 miles of shoreline can be viewed across Lubec Channel.

After visting the lighthouse, return to the parking lot and head straight for the **Coastal Trail.** This 4-mile round-trip route pierces the forest while staying close to the rocky outlets that weave in and out along the shore. As you walk on the soft moss, inhale the best air imaginable: the crisp smell of the forest mixed with the salty sea mist from the pounding waves below.

At **Gulliver's Hole,** the ocean waters surge upward against the cliffs and echo loudly. The harsh winds at **High Ledge** shape the trees,

Quoddy Head State Park

creating the perfect perch for a bald eagle when I ventured here last. Past Green Point, the trail continues for one additional mile to Carrying Place Cove. You can return via either Quoddy Head Road or the Coastal Trail.

TWO, IF BY SEA

Canoeing

If you yearn for the calmness of still waters, you can find it on four ponds and lakes in Acadia National Park that are definitely worth a paddle. Start with the park's largest body of water, **Long Pond,** with the help of **National Park Canoe** in Pond's End (207-244-5854). If you have your own boat, try **Seal Cove Pond, Jordan Pond,** and **Eagle Lake.** Because most of these bodies of water are deep, anglers will find cold-water fish like salmon, lake trout, and brook trout.

Fishing

With saltwater fish galore, surf-casting from the shore of the southern beaches is extremely popular. Stripers and blues (striped bass and blue-fish) are the most sought-after fish. Visitors to Acadia National Park will find brook trout, brown trout, and bass.

The main targets for deep-sea fishing are the bottom fish found 1 to 20 miles from shore. Cod are the most common catch, ranging from a few pounds to the occasional 70-pounder. Then there are the sleek, silver-gray pollocks and the wide-eyed haddocks. Charter boats often go after the trophy fish: giant tunas weighing 250 to 800 pounds, hal-ibut, and sharks.

More than 50 deep-sea charter operators run boats off the coast of Maine. Among those that come highly recommended is **Captain Barry Gibson** (Brown Brothers Wharf, Boothbay Harbor; 207-633-3416), with full-day charters for up to six people aboard *Shark IV.* On Mount Desert Island, **Captain Rick Savage** offers private charters for up to 10 anglers (207-276-3785).

L.L. Bean's **Outdoor Discovery School** in Freeport (888-552-3261) offers a highly regarded fly-fishing school.

Sailing

The stunning coastline of Maine is ideally suited for the sport of sail-ing. You can anchor in a hidden cove, stroll on a remote island, and sleep with seals by your window that evening. With more islands than the Caribbean or Polynesia, Maine includes two thousand pine-studded islands that attract sailors and adventurers from around the world. All are drawn to a rigorous test of their skills as they navigate through dense fog and sail the rough current, with the eventual reward of sunny skies and calm water.

Windjammers docked in Pulpit Harbor, North Haven

The most popular sailing route is between Penobscot and French-man Bay on Maine's midcoast. Among the finest anchorages are North Haven Pulpit Harbor, Islesboro, and Acadia's sister island Isle Au Haut. Northeast of Mount Desert Island, Machiasport and Buck's Harbor are a welcome throwback to an era in which lobster fishermen and sailors greeted one another like long-lost brothers as they passed.

If you plan to charter a boat without crew, you will need to book well in advance and have two boating references. The minimum rental time for bare boats is one week. **Hinckley Yacht Charters** (Bass Harbor Marine, Bass Harbor; 1-800-492-7245), on the southwestern shores of Mount Desert Island, offers 24 boats, ranging from a 34-foot Sabre to a 49-foot Hinckley Ketch. **Bay Island Yacht Charters** in Rockland (1-800-421-2492; www.sailme.com) offers eight bare boats, from a Bristol 27 to a Hylas 44. They also offer American Sailing Association–accredited instruction and day rentals.

If you want to taste the salt of the sea in the Northeast's top cruising ground and you don't have the experience to charter a sailboat on your own, try the next-best thing—a real 19th-century or early 20th-century windjammer. Most of the schooners docked in Rockland, Rockport, and Camden were legitimate working vessels in the early 1900s. Take, for example, the *Grace Bailey*. Built in 1882, the 123-foot ship sailed to the West Indies in the fruit trade and carried granite in New York to help build Grand Central Station. In 1990, Captain Ray Williams renovated the *Grace Bailey* for commercial travel, to accommodate 29 passengers and a crew of 6.

As a passenger aboard the *Grace Bailey,* you leave from the picture-perfect harbor of Camden and sail the waters of Penobscot Bay, where the boat traffic is light. Prevailing winds are strong, and the *Grace Bailey* is one of the fastest schooners in the fleet, cruising at a good seven knots. Captain Ray is happy to hand you the wheel if you want to steer the vessel. You'll pass islands of pine, and seals suntanning on granite outcroppings. In the distance the rising hills of Camden climb higher as they continue north to Acadia National Park. If you choose the weekend trip, you'll anchor under the stars in the calm waters of Pulpit Harbor on the island of North Haven or Dark Harbor on Islesboro. The five-day trips take you to Deer Isle and Acadia National Park. There's no better way to see Cadillac Mountain in the summer than from the water, far away from the crowds. At night, passengers sing sea chanties and dine on lobster. Call 888-692-7245 or visit www.mainewindjammercruises.com.

Scuba Diving

Mount Desert Island's **Harbor Divers** (Route 102A, Bass Harbor; 207-244-5751) goes on daily trips to the small islands and canyons in Frenchman Bay to view seals, porpoises, pink starfish, soft sponges, and other marine life that call the cool waters of Maine home.

Sea Kayaking

Maine is hands down the premier sea kayaking destination in New England. The hundreds of isles and inlets provide easy shelter from the nasty winds and waves. Add the Maine Island Trail to the equation and you have one of the finest sea kayaking venues in North America. With all the bays, protected coves, and islands to choose from, it's no wonder that seemingly half the SUVs in Maine are topped with 14- to 16-foot-long sea kayaks.

The Maine Island Trail—the Appalachian Trail of the sea—is a 325-mile waterway that hugs the coast from Portsmouth, New Hampshire, to northeastern Maine at Machias. Designed solely for kayaks and small sailboats, the trail weaves from pine-covered island to pine-covered island through saltwater tributaries, picture-postcard bays, and secluded harbors. These 80 islands, rarely seen by the public, are available only to small watercraft.

The trail was created through efforts of the Maine Bureau of Public Lands and the Maine Island Trail Association. Access to the privately owned islands is permitted only to members of the association, which you can join for $40. Paddlers normally require a month to cover the entire trail. Contact the association at P.O. Box C, Rockland, ME, 04841; 207-596-6456.

Frenchman Bay, Acadia National Park. *Distance:* 3–4.5 miles. *Time:* 4.5 hours. *Difficulty:* Moderate. *Directions:* Contact **Coastal Kayaking Tours** (48 Cottage Street, Bar Harbor; 207-288-9605).

Perhaps the best way to see Acadia National Park is to paddle a sea kayak around the islands of Frenchman Bay. Coastal Kayaking offers daily four-hour guided tours of the waters surrounding Acadia

National Park. They'll fit you for life jacket, sea skirt, and booties, and off you go with van and kayaks to the bar of Bar Harbor, a sand spit that juts out of town at low tide. Prior sea kayaking experience is not necessary.

Guides will teach you some basic strokes, help you get acclimated to your new mode of transportation, and then push you off into the wild blue yonder. With your group you'll cruise around the northern shores of Bar Island, where bright pink starfish lie on the rocks, and then continue around Sheep Porcupine Island, where porpoises and seals are often found playing. As you cross the main boat passage into Bar Harbor, you'll be rewarded with exquisite views of 1,530-foot Cadillac Mountain, the highest peak in Acadia National Park. Guides usually stop for a 15-minute break at The Hop, a small island at the northernmost tip of Long Porcupine Island, so you can stretch your legs before the return trip.

On the west side of Long Porcupine, the water can get choppy but should flatten out as you approach Burnt Porcupine Island. Here you'll find plump black guillemots divebombing into the water in search of food. You might also see loons lounging under the sun. You will cross the main passage once again and weave through the schooners and fishing boats anchored off the pier of Bar Harbor to return to terra firma.

Inn-to-Inn Sea Kayaking, mid-Maine coast. *Distance:* 7–8 miles per day. *Time:* 4 days. *Difficulty:* Moderate. *Directions:* Contact **H2Outfitters** (Orrs Island, 1-800-205-2925; www.h2outfitters.com).

As the fog receded, we were treated to a view of Maine's coastline few have seen since Winslow Homer captured it on his canvases over a century ago. The battering surf of the North Atlantic thrust against a boulder-strewn coastline, spewing foam high into the air. Juniper pines, dwarfed by gales, refused to budge from the land above. Protected in my shell of a kayak, I held onto a lobster buoy, not wanting to be sucked into the middle of the ocean's reunion with land. I veered toward the open water, following my group of propeller-style paddlers. We were joined by seals who popped their heads out of the water to see who these foolhardy creatures could be.

It was day three of a four-day inn-to-inn sea kayaking tour of Maine's midcoast, organized by H2Outfitters. While daily sightings of cormorants, ospreys, and seals were common, *Homo sapiens* were rarely seen or heard until we ventured out of our boats in the late afternoon to shower and dine at a sumptuous inn. It was the best of both worlds. During the day, we would kayak 7 or 8 miles along the rugged shores and remote islands of Maine. In the evening, after washing the salt from our bodies, we would dine on succulent lobster, steamed clams, blueberry cobbler, and other treats of a New England clambake and then plop down in a nearby bed.

Vast acres of farmland bordered both sides of the road as I drove south from congested Route 1 to our meeting point in South Harpswell, a small fishing village. I had chosen this trip because it was led by Jeff Cooper. Owner of H2Outfitters on Orrs Island for the past 20 years, Cooper and his wife Cathy Piffath are respected teachers of sea kayaking along the East Coast.

Within moments of arrival, each member of our group of 10, including some novices, jumped into the cubbyhole seat of a sea kayak. We grabbed our paddles and pushed off. Hiding behind his Grizzly Adams beard, Cooper is a bundle of hyperintensity on land. Get him in that ocean, however, with his favorite wooden paddle, and his stroke is fluid, meditative. Cooper reviewed the basic stroke of kayaking, where pushing is just as important as pulling the paddle through the water to create a rapid churning motion. Then we moved on to wet exits

Sea kayaking with Jeff Cooper of H2Outfitters

from the kayak, played with the tidal changes, and cruised over three-foot swells as the tip of the boat slammed against the waves.

The days on water were a blissful blur as the continuum of time seemed to flow with the current out to sea. Suspended halfway in the ocean, my head inches away from the water line, my paddling became almost Zenlike. I would drift into my own thoughts and then be drawn back into the group, usually by one of Cooper's raunchy jokes. A common sense of adventure brought us closer together, especially during times of danger. One late morning, the ubiquitous Maine fog limited visibility to less than 15 feet. We tried to cross the mile-wide Sheepscot River, but quickly retreated when we heard the roar of an unseen lobster boat.

Back on the wraparound veranda of the Grey Havens Inn in Georgetown, we waited for the fog to lift. Built in 1904, this turreted, gray-shingled inn and its mellow pine paneling (no flowered wallpaper here) is conducive to lounging. I moved back and forth on an Adirondack-style rocking chair, watching the Atlantic disrobe from its layers of haze. Someone planted a cool beer in my hands. Ahh, the life of an inn-to-inn sea kayaker.

A DAY AT THE BEACH

Swimming? Head to the Rhode Island beaches, Cape Cod, or Ogunquit in southern Maine. No one heads to the Maine coast north of Portland for a dip, unless you're a penguin or a puffin. Freezing is the word: You jump in for five seconds, scream, and then run out. Locals head to **Popham Beach State Park** in Phippsburg, or to **Reid State Park** in Georgetown (see "Walks and Rambles") where three separate beaches range in character from freezing ocean surf to protected backwaters that are good for kids. Good for kids with skin as thick as a walrus's, that is.

CAMPGROUNDS

Sparsely populated and virtually unspoiled, the camping facilities on the Maine coast rank as some of the best in the nation. This is especially true of the national and state park facilities. For further information on state parks, contact the **Maine Bureau of Parks and Recreation,** Station 22, Augusta, ME 04333; 207-287-3821. The following parks are listed generally from south to north, beginning just north of Portland.

Hermit Island Campground, Bath (207-443-2101). From Bath, head south on Route 209. At the junction of Routes 209 and 216, continue south on Route 216 to Hermit Island and the campground. The campground provides 275 sites (no hook-ups), hot showers, flush toilets, picnic tables, a boat launch, and canoe rentals. It's hard to top this campground, on a 225-acre private island where each spacious site is set in the woods on the shore of Casco Bay, a great place for sailors, sea kayakers, and boaters. The campground owns a 50-foot deep-sea fishing boat that sails daily for cod and tuna.

Ocean View Park Campground, Phippsburg (207-389-2564). From the junction of Routes 1 and 209 in Bath, drive 13 miles south on Route 209 to the campground. You'll find 48 sites (11 with full hook-ups, 31 with water and electricity), hot showers, flush toilets, fire places, and a store. Right next to the sandy shores of Popham Beach State Park and sitting at the very end of the Phippsburg Peninsula, the campground can make you feel like you're walking the plank off the mainland into the ocean. It's a great swimming and fishing locale.

Orrs Island Campground, Orrs Island (207-833-5595). From the junction of Routes 1 and 24 in Bath, drive 11 miles south on Route 24 to the campground. There are 70 sites (35 with full hook-ups, 18 with water and electricity), hot showers, flush toilets, fireplaces, a laundry facility, a store, boat mooring, and canoe rentals. This family-oriented campground sits on a bluff overlooking Harpswell Sound—great for sea kayaking. You can visit nearby H2Outfitters (see "Sea Kayaking") for a quick lesson.

Camp Seguin Ocean Camping, Georgetown (207-371-2777). From the junction of Routes 127 and 1 in Bath, take Route 127 south for 10 miles and bear right on Reid State Park Road. The campground is another 2 miles down the road. The facility provides 30 sites for tents (a few with water and electricity), hot showers, flush toilets, fireplaces, a limited store, a rec room, and a playground. Nestled in the evergreens on the rocky shores of Sheepscot Bay, the grounds are next door to Reid State Park (see "Walks and Rambles"). It's an ideal place for walkers and sea kayakers.

Camden Hills State Park, Camden (207-236-3109). Located just 2 miles north of Camden on Route 1. The park offers 112 sites (no hookups), hot showers, flush toilets, ice, and a playground. The park is ideally located for hikes to Mount Battie and Maiden Cliff. It's also close to the quaint town of Camden.

Warren Island State Park, Penobscot Bay (207-236-0849). This small state park is located on a 70-acre island in the heart of Penobscot Bay, only minutes away from Islesboro. There's one small hitch—you need your own boat or sea kayak to get here. There are 10 campsites, 2 Adirondack shelters, fresh drinking water, and pit toilets; docking facilities are available.

Blackwoods Campground, Acadia National Park. From the junction of Routes 3 and 233, head 5 miles south on Route 3. The campground provides 306 sites (no hook-ups), flush toilets, and fireplaces. The campground is open year-round. Reservations can be made at least eight weeks in advance from June 15 through September 15 by contacting the park at P.O. Box 177, Bar Harbor, ME 04609; 207-288-3338 or 207-288-3274. Situated in a forest of spruce and shrubs, the Blackwoods sites are conveniently located on the east side of Mount Desert Island, where trails lead up to the peak of Cadillac Mountain.

Seawall Campground, Acadia National Park. From the junction of Routes 102 and 102A, head 5 miles south on Route 102A. There are 212 sites (no hook-ups), flush toilets, and fireplaces. Open late May to late September. Contact the park at P.O. Box 177, Bar Harbor, ME 04609; 207-288-3338 or 207-244-3600. Seawall is on the island's quieter west side. The 212 drive-up or hike-in campsites are linked to shoreline and self-guided nature trails.

Mount Desert Campground, Mount Desert Island (207-244-3710). From Ellsworth, drive south on Route 3 onto Mount Desert Island. Follow Route 102/198 south, taking Route 198 south for 0.75 mile to the campground. The facility has 150 sites (some with water and electricity), hot showers, flush toilets, fireplaces, a store, a boat launch, and canoe rentals. Located at the tip of majestic Somes Sound, these well-spaced sites beneath the pines are centrally located to Acadia's hikes and walks.

Lamoine State Park, Ellsworth (207-667-4778). From the junction of Routes 1 and 184 in Ellsworth, head 10 miles southeast on Route 184. The facility provides 61 sites (no hook-ups), pit toilets, a playground, and a swimming area. Situated across Eastern Bay from Mount Desert Island, Lamoine State Park is the best alternative if Blackwoods, Seawall, and Mount Desert Campgrounds are booked solid. Many of the sites are on the water, only a few minutes' walk from Lamoine Beach.

Isle au Haut, Acadia National Park (P.O. Box 177, Bar Harbor, ME 04609; 207-288-3338). Eight miles south of Stonington, this island is accessible by mailboat (207-367-5193). Five Adirondack-style shelters at Duck Harbor, accommodating six people each, are available by reservation only. The charge is $25 to secure a site, but forms should be sent back on time (April 1). Camping is permitted in the shelters from mid-May through mid-October. In the shoulder season (mid-September through mid-June) you have to walk 5 miles from the town landing to Duck Harbor. Consider yourself fortunate if you've secured a spot in one of these lean-tos; it's a sea kayaking hot spot.

Cobscook Bay State Park, Sunset Coast (207-726-4412). From the junction of Routes 1 and 86 in Dennysville, head 6 miles south on Route 1. The park has 125 sites (no hook-ups), hot showers, pit toilets, a boat launch, and a playground. Many of the sites in this state park have views of Casco Bay. The facility is close to Quoddy State Park and to Cutler (see "Walks and Rambles" and "Birding").

Activity Index

Ballooning

Connecticut, Mystic
River Balloon Adventures, 15
Maine, Balloon Rides,
166
Massachusetts, Balloons
over New England,
122
Rhode Island, Kingston
Balloon Company,
46

Beaches

Connecticut, 35–39
Calf Pasture Beach,
35, 36
Compo Beach, 35, 37
Cove Island Park, 36
DuBois Beach, 39
Esker Point Beach, 39
Greenwich Point
Park, 35
Hammonasset Beach,
38
Jennings Beach,
37
Lighthouse Point Park,
37–38
Ocean Beach Park, 39
Penfield Beach, 37
Rickers Beach, 37
Rocky Neck State
Park, 38–39
Sherwood Island State
Park, 36
Silver Sands Beach, 37
Town Beach, 38
Maine, 181, 212
Footbridge Beach, 181
Fortune Rocks Beach,
181
Goose Rocks Beach,
181
Laudholm Beach, 181
Long Sands Beach,
181
Main Beach, 181
Old Orchard Beach,
181
Popham Beach State
Park, 212
Reid State Park, 212
Wells Beach, 181
Massachusetts, 112–15,
160–61
Cape Cod National
Seashore, 76, 112,
114
Crane Beach, 160
Demarest Lloyd State
Park, 161
Duxbury Beach,
161
Good Harbor Beach,
161
Great Misery Island,
161
Horseneck Beach, 161
Humarock Beach, 161
Long Beach, 160, 161
Nantasket Beach, 161
nudist, 114–15
Onset Beach, 161
Plum Island Beach,
160
Rexhame Beach, 161
Salisbury Beach, 160
Singing Beach, 161
White Horse Beach,
161
Wingaersheek Beach,
161
New Hampshire, 180–81

General Index

Books from The Countryman Press

EXPLORER'S GUIDES

The Blue Ridge and Smoky Mountains, Jim Hargan
Cape Cod, Martha's Vineyard, and Nantucket, Kim Grant
Connecticut, Barnett D. Laschever & Andi Marie Fusco
Massachusetts: The North Shore, South Coast, Central Massachusetts, and the Berkshires,
 Christina Tree & William Davis
The Best of the Hudson Valley and Catskill Mountains, Joanne Michaels &
 Mary-Margaret Barile
Maine, Christina Tree & Elizabeth Roundy Richards
Maryland, Leonard Adkins
New Hampshire, Christina Tree & Christine Hamm
Rhode Island, Phyllis Méras & Tom Gannon
Vermont, Christina Tree & Sally West Johnson

A SELECTION OF BOOKS ABOUT NEW ENGLAND

Backroad Bicycling in Connecticut, Andi Marie Fusco
Backroad Bicycling on Cape Cod, Martha's Vineyard, and Nantucket,
 Susan Milton and Kevin & Nan Jeffrey
Backroad Bicycling in Western Massachusetts, Andi Marie Fusco
Canoe Camping Vermont and New Hampshire Rivers, Roioli Schweiker
50 Hikes in Connecticut, David, Sue, & Gerry Hardy
50 Hikes in the Maine Mountains, Cloe Chunn
50 Hikes in Southern and Coastal Maine, John Gibson
50 Hikes in Massachusetts, Brian White and John Brady
50 More Hikes in New Hampshire, Daniel Doan & Ruth Doan MacDougall
50 Hikes in Vermont, Mary Deatt & Bob Lindemann for The Green Mountain Club
50 Hikes in the White Mountains, Daniel Doan & Ruth Doan MacDougall
Fishing Vermont's Streams & Lakes, Peter F. Cammann
Fly Fishing Boston, Terry Tessein
In-Line Skate New England, Cynthia & Thomas Lewis and Carolyn Bradley
Kayaking the Maine Coast, Dorcas Miller
Paddling Cape Cod, Shirley & Fred Bull
Paddling Southern New England, Ken Weber
Ponds and Lakes of the White Mountains, Steven D. Smith
Trout Streams of Northern New England, David Klausmeyer
Trout Streams of Southern New England, Tom Fuller
25 Bicycle Tours in Maine, Howard Stone
25 Bicycle Tours in Vermont, John Freidin
25 Mountain Bike Tours in Massachusetts, Robert S. Morse
Walks & Rambles on Cape Cod & the Islands, Ned Friary and Glenda Bendure
Walks & Rambles in Rhode Island, Ken Weber
Waterfalls of the White Mountains, Bruce, Doreen, and Daniel Bolnick
Weekend Walks Along the New England Coast, John Gibson

We offer many more books in hiking, fly-fishing, paddling, travel, nature, and other
subjects. Our books are available at bookstores and outdoor stores everywhere. For
more information or a free catalog, please call 1-800-245-4151 or write to us at The
Countryman Press, P.O. Box 748, Woodstock, VT 05091. You can find us on the
Internet at www.countrymanpress.com